JOE'S PALACE
and
CAPTURING MARY

also featuring A REAL SUMMER

Stephen Poliakoff, born in December 1952, was appointed writer
in residence at the National Theatre for 1976 and the same year won
the *Evening Standard*'s Most Promising Playwright Award for *Hitting
Town* and *City Sugar*. He has also won a BAFTA Award for the Best
Single Play for *Caught on a Train* in 1980, the *Evening Standard*'s Best
British Film Award for *Close My Eyes* in 1992, The Critics' Circle
Best Play Award for *Blinded by the Sun* in 1996 and the Prix Italia
and the Royal Television Society Best Drama Award for *Shooting the
Past* in 1999. His plays and films include *Clever Soldiers* (1974),
The Carnation Gang (1974), *Hitting Town* (1975), *City Sugar* (1975),
Heroes (1975), *Strawberry Fields* (1977), *Stronger than the Sun* (1977),
Shout Across the River (1978), *American Days* (1979), *The Summer Party*
(1980), *Bloody Kids* (1980), *Caught on a Train* (1980), *Favourite Nights*
(1981), *Soft Targets* (1982), *Runners* (1983), *Breaking the Silence* (1984),
Coming in to Land (1987), *Hidden City* (1988), *She's Been Away* (1989),
Playing with Trains (1989), *Close My Eyes* (1991), *Sienna Red* (1992),
Century (1994), *Sweet Panic* (1996), *Blinded by the Sun* (1996), *The
Tribe* (1997), *Food of Love* (1998), *Talk of the City* (1998), *Remember
This* (1999), *Shooting the Past* (1999), *Perfect Strangers* (2001) for
which he won the Dennis Potter Award at the 2002 BAFTAs and
Best Writer and Best Drama at the Royal Television Society Awards,
and *The Lost Prince* (2003), winner of three Emmy Awards in 2005
including Outstanding Mini Series. His most recent work for the BBC
includes *Friends and Crocodiles* (2006) and *Gideon's Daughter* (also
2006) which won two Golden Globes and a Peabody Award in 2007.

JOE'S PALACE

and

CAPTURING MARY

also featuring A REAL SUMMER

Stephen Poliakoff

Introduced by the author

Methuen Drama

Published by Methuen Drama 2007

10 9 8 7 6 5 4 3 2 1

Methuen Drama
A & C Black Publishers Limited
38 Soho Square
London WID 3HB
www.acblack.com

ISBN: 978 0 713 68811 5

A CIP catalogue record for this book is available from
the British Library

Typeset by Country Setting, Kingsdown, Kent
Printed and bound in Great Britain by
CPI Cox & Wyman, Reading, RG1 8EX

Caution

Contents

Introduction

My father knew a lot of rich men. They seemed to populate much of his life even though he himself was often in severe financial difficulties. Throughout my childhood his manufacturing business teetered on the edge of bankruptcy before it finally flowered in the 1970s, but this did not deter him from mingling with the very rich.

One particular millionaire interested my father greatly. He lived near us in central London and was often invited over to our house for a glass of sherry. He was a very short man, with a very loud voice, and I found him rather terrifying. As a child I had very little idea about how this man had made his money, but I did know that he owned this beautiful building in Piccadilly which at night glowed like a big ship. My father frequently found an excuse to drive past it and every time pointed it out to me. I stared at it so often from the back of the car that I knew a lot of its rooms by heart. Nothing ever seemed to go on in this building, but it was always spotless, always being cleaned.

The image of a large house suspended in time, unoccupied but fully furnished, lying in wait for something to happen inside it, has stayed with me since I was a child and was the starting point of *Joe's Palace*. We all probably share to some extent my father's fascination with the houses of the wealthy and what lies beyond those immaculate stucco exteriors in Mayfair and Belgravia. At one time, not so long ago, this country was run from these London mansions as the political and aristocratic elite entertained each other within their walls at a constant series of lavish parties. Today there are more

billionaires in London than in any other city on earth and
many of them own mysterious large properties that it is impossible to penetrate, even though some of the houses have
been empty for many years.

So I started with a house. Normally when I am working
on a story I begin with a character and work outwards from
that, but in the case of *Joe's Palace* I began with the interior
of the London mansion and then various characters started
to reverberate through the empty house. For some time I had
wanted to see if I could write a story about loneliness which
wasn't mournful or full of bittersweet yearning but had energy
and danger. Loneliness consumes so many people at different stages of their lives and yet it remains unmentionable, a
stigma that nobody should own up to. A large London house,
beautiful but inexplicably empty, gave me my way into a story
of urban loneliness.

Once I had the house as a starting point and was moving
around it in my mind in search of characters, I had the idea
of seeing all the action through the eyes of an adolescent boy,
the son of one of the cleaners. If he became the centre of the
story I felt the situation would become fresher, more univer-
sal and not too rarefied.

Unless we have been very lucky in our adolescence, we have
all, at some time, experienced moments of deep isolation
when confidence and adult certainty seemed particularly un-
obtainable. This was the prism through which I wanted to
view all the action. But Joe is not a surly adolescent, he pos-
sesses a gentle empathy and this allows the adults in the story
to open up to him.

In *Joe's Palace*, we see three different characters experiencing a sense of isolation: Joe himself, the billionaire Elliot,
and Charlotte, who is conducting an affair with a young cabinet minister, Richard.

For Charlotte the house is initially a place for escape, somewhere convenient for Richard and her to meet. Their affair

brings life back into the empty building, and through Joe's eyes they seem a glamorous almost magical couple. Later in the story, when Charlotte realises the ephemeral nature of her love affair, the house becomes a place of refuge for her, as she sits alone in a room watching a silent television, contemplating her life.

In Elliot's case the house is a disquieting place. It resonates with memories from his childhood and the presence of his dead father. Elliot instinctively feels there is something wrong with how his secretive father made his fortune and he senses that he cannot break free of the past until he has confronted it. But his efforts to discover the truth about his father have led nowhere and, as the years have gone by, he has shrunk into a shy withdrawn world. He is literally stuck, unable to get any momentum into his life.

Many writers at some stage in their careers experience a case of agoraphobia when it seems particularly difficult to go out of the front door and face the world, and this is one of the reasons I wanted to write about Elliot. The other more powerful reason was that through my recent work I had been searching for different ways to write about Nazism and the Holocaust. In both *Shooting the Past* and *Perfect Strangers* there were stories that came from that time. In *Joe's Palace* the source of Elliot's father's fortune also leads us back to what happened in Europe in the 1930s and 1940s. As a dramatist I am haunted by the paradox that the further we get away from those times, as each decade passes, the nearer they seem to be.

In *Joe's Palace* I wanted to dramatise one of the countless incidents of humiliation that the Jewish population suffered in full view of normal German citizens as they went about their business on a Sunday afternoon. The indifference of the non-Jewish population to what was happening in front of them in this particular Berlin park becomes a metaphor for the indifference of the whole of Europe. They knew what was happening but they either watched or turned their backs. We are all still dealing with the consequences of this every day of our lives in the twenty-first century.

When writing *Capturing Mary* I also drew on my childhood. In 1958, when the story is set, I was five years old, and the most important images in my life at that time were the lines of uniformed nannies sitting with their prams in Holland Park, the incredibly bright red strawberry ice-creams that were served in Lyon's Corner Houses, and my mother dressed in the romantic long dresses of the period staring down at me in bed before she swept off to some social occasion. But even as a small child I remember sensing an unsettling atmosphere hovering beneath the formal surface of late fifties life. Certain adults I encountered were full of barely concealed rage which they could not even manage to hide successfully from a five-year-old child.

This was a time of vicious hierarchy; the British class system that had partially melted during the Second World War reformed with a vengeance and sat like a suffocating permanent crust on top of all forms of fifties life. A lot of people were not able to lead the emotional or sexual lives they wanted to, whether it was because they were gay or because they were trapped in a marriage that no longer worked but from which they were unable to break free because of the stigma that divorce held. Women of course were still expected to stay at home and look after the children; the emancipation the war had brought had all but vanished.

There was a very powerful feeling of frustration in the air, of trapped energy. It was an environment in which certain people could exercise power over others, usually those younger than them, in a wilful and sometimes purely sadistic way.

Naturally as a small child most of this passed me by, but later on I would encounter many adults who had been scarred by this time and were now taking it out on others. Several of these characters were to leave an indelible impression on me, especially in my late teens when I first started writing. They ranged from moderately insane schoolmasters, to predatory theatre directors, to distinctly sinister elderly drama critics who wined and dined me as a very young playwright.

In *Capturing Mary* we see this world by experiencing the London mansion in its heyday. The older Mary enters the house in the present and as she roams its empty rooms the memories and ghosts of that time come flooding back. When her younger self enters the house in 1958 she brings with her the whiff of change, of a more classless world, the fearlessness of youth, a sense of the sixties before that decade had been born. She is very much of the generation that was beginning to explore new worlds in the theatre and was soon to do the same in British cinema, escaping the cosy southern world of Pinewood Studios as films discovered the industrial heartlands of Britain.

Although Young Mary is clearly a progressive character, she is not without a deep curiosity about the rich and famous who attend the soirées at the grand London mansion. It is this curiosity, a natural requirement for a writer, that leads to her collision with Greville.

Greville is a reactionary figure, somebody who is very comfortable within the elite of the late fifties. But he is also a man of intelligence and a certain instinct, and he realises that Young Mary may well be a harbinger of change, of a new, more democratic era. He wants to befriend her, preferably to seduce her, but failing that to charm her and in some way control her. He feels that if he can neutralise people like Mary there is a future for him in the different climate that he can sense is coming.

Young Mary's problem is that she is too confident, too fearless. She feels she can handle Greville, she doesn't realise when she defies him there can only be one outcome. For this was a time when if you took on the establishment your career could be finished overnight in a way that is unimaginable now. Certain British film actors, some of them movie stars, found themselves ostracised when they fell out publicly with powerful forces within the industry. So if celebrities at the time could be put out of work, a young female writer would have been even more vulnerable.

Mary finds it impossible to shake off her traumatic encounter with Greville; it haunts her whole life. Clearly a loss of confidence in her own ability, which often follows early success, is one of the factors that contribute to her decline. The audience can make up their own minds how much this is due to Greville's actions and how much to Mary's own indiscipline and indulgence. But one of the things I wanted to show in the story was how when the mature had absolute power over the young they could not just damage young people's careers but they could also dwell in their victim's psyche for many years afterwards.

When Mary seems to see Greville in the park at the end of the film it is not a 'real ghost' but a manifestation of extreme depression, a hallucination born out of despair.

I met several Grevilles in my early career who were even more dangerous than the predatory theatre directors or the spooky drama critics of my adolescence. One encounter with a famous producer in his London house was so disquieting it still casts a slight chill even now. It is difficult to analyse exactly why I felt such a powerful sense of evil as I sat opposite this man in his comfortable sitting room which overlooked the Thames. He was offering me a job, a job I knew I would have to decline, but I also realised that by saying no to him I was going to turn him into an implacable enemy. As he talked I had the bizarre feeling that if I wasn't very careful my whole career would be in jeopardy. Somehow I extricated myself from the room and I didn't stop running until I was several streets away. Later I was told this neatly turned-out gentleman had single-handedly destroyed several careers.

The hierarchical world that I was born into and experienced as a child and a young adult did not melt overnight, for my own experiences of it were in the 1970s. The Grevilles of the world took a long time dying as they trailed their fifties bitterness, their sense of disappointment and rage, into several other decades. But of course the first sign of their demise began in the sixties, a decade that Mary could have truly flourished in. Her tragedy is that by the time she reaches the sixties her confidence has been ripped out of her. As Mary says herself, 'It rarely pays to be in the vanguard of things, one is superseded very quickly.'

In *A Real Summer*, the short play that accompanies *Capturing Mary*, I've experimented for the first time in my career in writing a prequel. It is difficult to dramatise a writer's voice in a single film, especially if that story has quite a strong narrative drive as is the case of *Capturing Mary*. So I thought I would see if I could add to the audience's understanding of Young Mary by creating this additional work.

The story I hope both helps to evoke that pivotal year 1958, the last season the debs were presented to the Queen, and also shows Young Mary in vivid, confident form before she encounters the sinister Greville. In the play Young Mary tells the story of her unexpected friendship with a young aristocrat Geraldine. When we first meet Geraldine, as described by Young Mary in her column, she seems frivolous, vulnerable and ignorant. But by the end of the story, during their long phone call together, we realise Geraldine is the more worldly one, that she is right to be fearful for the future of Young Mary, who despite all her sophistication does not realise the strength of the world that she so freely criticises.

In these three works I have attempted to write about the present and the past in a way that I have not done before. *Joe's Palace* mingles my more recent measured style with some of the staccato rhythms of my early work in a blend that I hope is new. *Capturing Mary* is a much darker, more pitiless work than I have written before, and *A Real Summer* is stylistically different to anything I have previously attempted.

These works were made during a very eventful and difficult year for British television, when public service broadcasting was hit by a seemingly never-ending stream of 'scandals' and experienced something of a collective loss of confidence.

The future for television drama is clearly very much caught up in what happens to the major broadcasting institutions in this country. Nobody quite knows what to expect next. The new technology, the digital switchover, the multitude of choice available to the audience, make the future even more impossible to predict than usual. I myself have no idea what will happen to television drama and the authored work in particular. In the short term it will still be with us, but who knows what will happen in five years' time.

I only know it has been a very exciting period of my career, writing and directing shows for the most powerful medium on earth, and being able to reach so many people. As always I have been motivated by the desire to try to create works that will somehow last, even though they have been made for a medium that is frequently dubbed ephemeral. Time naturally will be the judge of this, and while I am waiting for its verdict I will be watching, and no doubt participating in, the almighty tussle that is going to ensue over the future of British broadcasting.

Stephen Poliakoff
September 2007

JOE'S PALACE

Joe's Palace was produced by TalkbackTHAMES for BBC Television and HBO Films and was first screened in November 2007. The cast was as follows:

Elliot	Michael Gambon
Joe Dix	Danny Lee Wynter
Richard Reece	Rupert Penry-Jones
Charlotte	Kelly Reilly
Tina	Rebecca Hall
Dave	Clive Russell
Mrs Hopkins	Carolyn Pickles
Sally Dix	Caroline Lee Johnson
Jason	Alfie Allen
Whittle	Celyn Jones
Patricia	Michelle MacErlean
Foster	Graham Padden
Young Mr Graham	Max Dowler
Middle-Aged Woman	Sarah Crowden
Laarni	Lourdes Faberes
Party Woman	Belinda Stewart Wilson
Inventor	Sam Bond
Dark Lady	Olivia Carruthers
Crying Woman	Kerry Lyn Hamilton
Antiques Expert	Geoffrey Munn

Writer/Director Stephen Poliakoff
Producer Deborah Jones
Music Adrian Johnston
Director of Photography Danny Cohen
Film Editor Clare Douglas
Production Designer Mark Leese

EXT. LONDON STREET. DAY

Credit sequence.

A swirl of commuters coming towards us across one of the bridges over the Thames. City workers hurrying to be at work on time.

A long-lens shot. In the middle of the throng is JOE, *a chunky boy of about seventeen. He is walking towards us steadily, much more slowly than the rush-hour crowd all around him, who brush past him, overtake him. All the time he keeps coming towards us, thinking his own thoughts.*

He has unruly hair, and is wearing a T-shirt, a shabby jacket, jeans and trainers.

We pick him up on another street walking his steady, slightly rolling walk. People scurrying past him, occasionally banging into him. JOE *suddenly stops, having seen something on the pavement. He stands stock-still for a moment as people dodge past him. He then bends down and picks up a child's small hairbrush. He stares at it for a moment. He continues his walk, holding it, letting it dangle from his hand, before dropping it into a litter bin.*

We follow his progress through a series of London streets as the credits play. JOE *looks neither left nor right, but ambles towards us in his chunky trainers, deep in thought. The shots are leading us into a street of houses in Mayfair, huge, tall town houses, an exclusive enclave of gentlemen's clubs, immensely expensive private houses and discreet upmarket offices.*

As JOE *moves along this street, he stops again. An empty supermarket trolley is standing abandoned on the pavement, looking rather incongruous in this wealthy street.* JOE *peers at it for a moment, standing stock-still, then moves on.*

EXT. THE LARGE TOWN HOUSE. DAY

JOE *arrives at the front door of a very large house. A London mansion with a fine nineteenth-century exterior, it has a formidable black door with a sliding panel in it, so whoever is calling can be interrogated without opening the door.*

JOE *rings the bell. The credits finish.*

*The panel slides back, and a man in his late fifties (*DAVE*) stares rather ferociously through the panel. He has a strong Glaswegian accent.*

DAVE: What do you want?

JOE: I have an appointment.

DAVE: With whom?

JOE *looks unfazed by* DAVE*'s intimidating presence.*

JOE: Not sure . . . my mother works here.

DAVE: And who's your mother?

JOE: Sally . . . Mrs Dix.

DAVE *opens the big door.*

INT. THE LARGE HOUSE. DAY

JOE *enters a large hallway, a dark grand room with a gleaming, polished marble floor. An impressive staircase sweeps up to the other floors – cleaners are polishing its banisters – and in the distance passages lead off towards the cavernous interior of the house. A couple more cleaners are washing the marble floor. There are no carpets on the ground floor. The building gleams like the interior of an ocean liner. The dark interior is brightened by there being flowers everywhere in elegant slender vases.*

DAVE *grunts at* JOE.

DAVE: You better come with me . . .

DAVE *heads off down one of the dark passages; in his hand is a large bunch of keys which clink as he walks.* JOE *stares at the cleaners kneeling on the big staircase.*

JOE: Does he live here all on his own?

DAVE: Mr Graham doesn't live here, he's across the road, number 36.

JOE (*peering down one of the other passages*): Who lives here then?

DAVE *glances back at* JOE *over his shoulder. He smiles.*

DAVE: No one . . . !

INT. KITCHEN. DAY

JOE *follows* DAVE *into a large old-fashioned kitchen with an Aga, and lots of pots and pans hanging up. Everything is very clean. In the middle of the kitchen, washing glasses at the sink, is* JOE*'s mother,* SALLY. *She is a woman in her early forties with a rather harassed appearance.*

SALLY: There you are, Joe! And exactly on time . . . I told everybody you would be on time!

DAVE (*grunting*): Didn't tell me . . .

SALLY: He is a very punctual boy . . . he never hurries, but he is never late.

A sharp-faced woman in her fifties, MRS HOPKINS, *enters the kitchen. She has a very neat appearance; her demeanour is a little distant and impersonal but not unpleasant.*

SALLY (*calling out to her*): Here he is, Jean! Just like I said.

MRS HOPKINS: So you're Joe?

JOE *nods, but doesn't feel it is necessary to say anything.*

SALLY: Joe, say hello to Mrs Hopkins . . . ! He doesn't talk a lot, do you, Joe! He's not shy or anything, but he doesn't speak much . . .

JOE *is looking around the kitchen as his mother is talking. He sees piles of old newspaper and colour magazines carefully stacked in bundles in the corner. He stares at the covers of the magazines: they are from the 1960s.*

MRS HOPKINS: Well, Joe, as it happens Mr Graham is here today which is a real piece of luck . . . So I am going to take you to him.

She indicates for JOE *to follow her. As* JOE *moves,* DAVE
looms over him and grins.

DAVE: Be careful . . .

INT./EXT. PASSAGE AND COURTYARD. DAY
A powerful track through the house as JOE *follows* MRS HOPKINS,
his mother and DAVE *along the passages. He is a few paces
behind them and refuses to hurry. We catch just fleeting glimpses
of the interiors of the main reception rooms.* JOE *suddenly decides
to stop when he catches sight of something in one of these rooms:
a long line of shoes going back decades in fashion, arranged
neatly along the length of one of the walls.* JOE *stands in the
doorway staring at the shoes. His mother's voice is calling.*

SALLY: Joe . . . you must keep up!

We cut to JOE *reaching them. From his point of view we
see the internal courtyard around which the house is built.
It is full of flowering shrubs. Through the window he first
catches a glimpse of* ELLIOT GRAHAM *sitting in the sun
on a small bench. He is in a jacket but wearing jeans. He
has a seemingly benign manner, a gentle smile on his face.
Sitting next to him is an efficient-looking accountant
figure in a business suit,* FOSTER.

ELLIOT *is in the middle of eating a sandwich.* JOE
stares fascinated as ELLIOT *carefully picks the pieces of
salami out of the sandwich, puts the bread to one side,
folds the piece of salami neatly and then eats it.*

MRS HOPKINS: Mr Graham . . . this is Joe. He will be on
the front door in the afternoons between one and
six . . . to give Dave a bit of a break, after all these
years.

DAVE *grunts in the shadows. Everybody is keeping a very
respectful distance from* ELLIOT, *talking to him from
across the courtyard.*

ELLIOT *looks up, gives* JOE *a little smile.*

SALLY: He's very reliable, Mr Graham . . . Everybody
always says Joe's really punctual . . . his school reports
and everything!

ELLIOT: Excellent . . . (*He stares straight at* JOE *for a
moment.*) I am sure he will do. (ELLIOT *turns to the
second half of his sandwich, and takes the salami out of
the bread. He then looks back at* JOE.) You know what to
do?

JOE, *his manner unafraid, unhurried, doesn't immediately
reply. He is watching the salami and* ELLIOT.

SALLY (*prompting him*): Joe . . . !

JOE: Yes . . . I know what to do.

ELLIOT: And you'll write down everybody that calls? Keep
a record for me?

JOE: Sure . . . I can do that.

INT./EXT. SOUTH LONDON. EVENING

We cut to inside JOE*'s home. We start inside the cramped
interior.* JOE *is standing on the small balcony of their flat in
a block of low-rise housing on a south London estate. He is
staring out across the concrete playground spread below him.*

*His mother is sitting on the end of her bed doing her make-up.
She is dressed to go out for the night.*

SALLY *stares at herself in the mirror.*

SALLY: I look so tired, don't I . . . ? I so want to look good
tonight. Do I seem really old and tired, Joe?

She looks up at JOE *on the balcony.*

SALLY: Joe . . . ?!

JOE (*turns*): No. You don't.

SALLY *smiles.*

SALLY: You did really well today . . . just the clothes,
maybe, you could have looked a little smarter. When
you go tomorrow – you put your best clothes on,

you'll remember? (*She checks her make-up.*) It's great
you got the job though! The money's not bad, too. (*She
laughs.*) Keep you off the streets – not that I have ever
had to worry about that with you, Joe . . . You won't
see Mr Graham again anyway, probably. Not for a
long time. None of us see him much. We clean every
day and the place is spotless . . . but nobody uses it!
Hardly ever . . . occasionally he has a meeting there . . .
As his mother is talking, JOE *watches three kids of his age
crossing the playground, talking together, laughing. Then
they see him and immediately start mimicking him, doing
his plodding rolling walk, screaming, 'The weirdo's out
again!' They make monkey noises and grunts, and move
in an absurd way, like Neanderthals.* JOE *watches them,
totally impassive.*

INT./EXT. THE LARGE HOUSE. DAY
*We cut to the panel in the front door sliding open. And then
we cut to outside and see* JOE*'s face staring out at the world
through the big door.*

*His eyes flick up the street. He sees the supermarket trolley
has moved along the pavement; a smart passer-by skirts round
it like it is a diseased object.* JOE *shuts the panel. He glances
behind him into the hall: the cleaners are on the stairs polishing.
Deep in the building there is the sound of hoovering.*

There is a loud clanging: the front doorbell rings. JOE *slides
the panel back. A middle-aged* WOMAN *is standing in front of
the door; behind her is the supermarket trolley. She points
angrily at he trolley.*

WOMAN: Does this belong here?!
JOE: No.
WOMAN (*her tone getting angrier*): Well, do you know whose
it is?

JOE *stares at her, totally unfazed.*

JOE: No.

WOMAN: Well, you'd think somebody in the neighbourhood would deal with it! (*Pointedly.*) Would remove it! (*Her voice rising.*) Something has to be done, doesn't it?!

JOE *just stares straight at her.*

JOE: It can't come in here.

He slides the panel in the door shut.

INT. JOE'S BEDROOM. EVENING

We cut to JOE*'s small bedroom in the south London flat. He is sitting on his bed with a Discman skipping tracks. He is staring across at the photos on his wall: one is a big black-and-white photo of a wombat, a sturdy fat specimen staring back at him. On another wall is a rather beautiful pin-up of a female singer.*

The wombat and JOE *exchange looks.*

INT./EXT. THE LARGE HOUSE. DAY

Rain is pouring down. JOE *stares out through the panel into the empty street. The rain buckets down. No one is around.*

He looks back across the marble hall. A young Asian woman is arranging the flowers lovingly in their slender vases. He gives her a little, rather awkward nod. His mother is moving along a passage on the first floor.

JOE *looks back into the street, just in time to see* ELLIOT GRAHAM*'s large car, a very superior Mercedes, draw up outside the house opposite. A uniformed chauffeur is driving.* ELLIOT *gets out briskly before the car has hardly stopped and makes for his front door. He is dressed in a tracksuit and trainers.*

ELLIOT *suddenly stops and sees his shoelace is undone. He bends down in the middle of the pavement and starts doing it up even though he is getting soaked and is just outside his front door. The chauffeur rushes out of the car, perturbed at seeing*

ELLIOT *getting soaked. He desperately unfurls an umbrella, but* ELLIOT *waves him away, telling him he's fine.* ELLIOT *finishes doing his lace up, seemingly completely oblivious of the rain.*

JOE *is watching this, very intrigued.* ELLIOT *then moves off into his house and disappears.*

INT. KITCHEN. LATE AFTERNOON
The rain is still pouring down. JOE *is sitting in the empty kitchen, writing slowly in a notebook. We hear his voice as he writes.*

JOE (*voice-over*): Forgot to write anything yesterday. No callers today. Saw Mr Graham doing up his shoelaces in the rain.
There is a loud knocking on the front door. A sharp incisive knock.

INT./EXT. THE HALL. AFTERNOON
We cut to JOE *sliding back the panel. He sees a beady, intelligent face staring back at him: a man in his thirties* (RICHARD) *with a mercurial, rather charismatic smile and a playful, charming manner. The rain is still pouring down.*

RICHARD: Is Dave here?
JOE: No.
RICHARD: Right . . . (*Charming smile.*) And who are you?
JOE: I am here for Dave, in the afternoons.
RICHARD: Really? You are here for Dave? Can I come in?
JOE: No.
RICHARD (*laughs*): No? . . . Just like that? Don't worry, I am not a burglar . . . (*He grins, indicating the cleaners just packing up behind* JOE.) They know me . . .
RICHARD waves at the Asian girl and she nods and waves back.

JOE: Why do you want to come in?

RICHARD: I have got an appointment over the road with
Mr Graham and I am a little early . . .

JOE *sees there is a large car parked outside with a driver
in it.* RICHARD *follows* JOE*'s look.*

RICHARD: And my driver wants to have a smoke . . .

INT. HALL. LATE AFTERNOON
We cut to RICHARD *standing opposite* JOE *in the marble hall.*
The cleaners are getting ready to leave.

RICHARD (*smiles*): You're great at security. You're even
more difficult to get past than Dave. I am Richard
Reece. (*He holds out his hand.*) I am a member of the
government . . . (*He grins.*) You may want to throw me
back out in the rain now.

JOE *just stares at him.*

RICHARD: And you are?

JOE: I am Joe.

RICHARD (*smiles warmly*): Hello, Joe. (*He turns.*) I never
can get over these flowers . . . all these fresh flowers
every time I come . . . (*He grins.*) Not that I have been
allowed in here that often! And Dave never lets me
get past the hall . . . (*He smiles at* JOE.) Can I look at
the garden . . . ?

INT./EXT. GARDEN. LATE AFTERNOON
We cut to RICHARD *and* JOE *standing on the edge of the
courtyard garden.*

RICHARD: Amazingly well attended . . . a beautiful oasis . . .
You'd never guess all this was here from out in the
street! (*Charming smile.*) I hate buildings I can't get

into . . . I am very nosy. (*Suddenly.*) Have you ever been upstairs?

JOE: No.

RICHARD: Neither have I! (*Sharp smile.*) Shall we take a look?

INT. PASSAGEWAYS AND BEDROOMS. LATE AFTERNOON
RICHARD *moving along the upstairs passage, looking into each interior. He tries each door; some are locked, some are open. He sees bedrooms, beautifully furnished, as in an exclusive hotel.*

RICHARD: Amazing! Absolutely amazing . . . all these rooms perfectly tended! . . . Flowers of course . . . (*Grinning, moving into one of the en-suite bathrooms.*) Fresh soap. (*Pointing.*) Slippers, even . . . ! Bathrobes! It's spotless . . . And it's only ever seen by the cleaners. . . !

JOE (*watching him closely*): Yes.

RICHARD: It's like a big ship about to set off somewhere, isn't it . . . ?

JOE: Yes.

RICHARD *stares at* JOE *for a moment.*

RICHARD (*grins*): No passengers, though!

JOE: No.

INT./EXT. HALLWAY AND STREET. LATE AFTERNOON
We cut to the hallway. RICHARD *has the front door open. He turns back to* JOE *as he is about to leave.*

RICHARD: So, Joe . . . very good to meet you. You should get them to arrange a desk for you, with a good chair and a phone, maybe . . . like a proper concierge!

JOE *looks bemused by this.*

RICHARD: Like a proper security person. (*He smiles.*) Which you undoubtedly are.

JOE *watches* RICHARD *cross the street and ring the bell of* ELLIOT's *house, number 36. The door opens.* RICHARD *gives* JOE *a little wave and disappears inside.*

INT. THE LARGE HOUSE. DAY
We cut to MRS HOPKINS *walking through pools of sunlight dotting the dark downstairs passage. She comes into the hall. There is* JOE *sitting at a fine desk, facing the front door. He is sitting on a tall, high-backed chair. Displayed on the desk he has a notebook and a mobile phone.*

MRS HOPKINS: You like your new desk, Joe?

JOE *is arranging a series of pencils in a line on the desk.*

JOE: It's fine.

We cut to later that day. It is the end of the afternoon. A stormy evening. It is very dark in the hall. Everybody is leaving sharp at six o'clock. JOE *is putting all his pencils away and getting ready to leave.*

DAVE is standing, in silhouette, across the other side of the hall.

The last person leaves. JOE *moves to follow.*

DAVE: Where do you think you're going?

JOE (*startled*): It's six o'clock.

DAVE: You need to stay a while.

JOE *hesitates.*

DAVE: And that's an order. (*His voice is full of tension and rather frightening. It cannot be contradicted.*) Come here, Joe . . . (*He raises his voice.*) COME ON!

JOE *moves towards him slowly very watchfully.*

DAVE: Don't be afraid . . . (*Then, his tone intense.*) It's just you can't leave tonight.

He suddenly moves off, the bunch of keys rattling in his hand.

DAVE: Follow me . . .

JOE remains stock-still in the hall. DAVE turns, his voice softer.

DAVE: Follow me . . .

JOE doesn't move. DAVE disappears from view. There is suddenly the sound of crockery being smashed and then again even louder, china being shattered coming from further down the passage. Then there is a loud cry.

JOE moves towards the sound. He finds DAVE in the kitchen surrounded by many pieces of broken china. As JOE enters, DAVE flings another plate onto the floor and then another against the wall. They both smash.

DAVE: You've got to stay for a while to stop me breaking things . . .

JOE is staring at DAVE. He's keeping his distance but he's intrigued, not afraid.

JOE: What's the matter?

DAVE: That's a good question, Joe . . .

It is almost dark in the kitchen now. DAVE smiles.

You've not been on the roof, have you, Joe . . . ?

JOE (*startled*): On the roof? Of here? No.

DAVE: I think that's where we've got to go . . .

EXT. THE ROOF OF THE LARGE HOUSE. NIGHT
Cut to DAVE standing on the flat roof of the house staring out across the London rooftops, the tall chimneys and ventilation units forming a surreal landscape. The roofs of the jumble of buildings of central London.

We see DAVE in wide shot at first, standing very near the edge. JOE keeps his distance.

DAVE: Come on, you can come closer than that! Don't be scared . . . (*Slight grin.*) Only one of us can go over tonight – and it probably won't be you . . .

JOE *can't tell if he is joking around or not. He moves a little closer, but still keeps his distance.* DAVE *is rattling the keys as he gets even closer to the edge.*

DAVE: Once you're here, working in this house, they never want to sack you . . . They don't like change. Didn't want me to leave – so they brought you along to make my life easier . . . (*Heartfelt.*) BUT I'VE GOT TO GET OUT OF HERE, JOE! When his father was alive – it was different. This place was fun! Parties twice a week! But now . . . (*He stares across the rooftops. He suddenly turns, staring at* JOE.) Don't be fooled by Mr Graham either . . . his bumbling act. He was in the army – hard to believe, I know, but he was! Special Unit! Killed people with his bare hands . . . Be careful . . . he can be a very frightening guy, Joe. (*He stares straight at* JOE, *intense.*) Sometimes . . . a really terrifying fellow . . .

JOE *meets his gaze.*

JOE: I'll remember . . .

DAVE: You can go now!

JOE *hesitates.*

DAVE: Go on!

JOE *begins to move away across the roof.* DAVE *smiles.*

DAVE: Just don't look back . . . Don't, Joe!

We track with JOE *as he leaves.* JOE *in the foreground,* DAVE *calling to him in the back of shot, right on the edge of the roof.*

DAVE: Don't look back.

JOE *doesn't look back.*

INT. THE LARGE HOUSE. DAY

DAVE's *large bunch of keys are placed sharply on a table. We cut wide to see we are in* MRS HOPKINS' *housekeeper's room.* JOE *is standing in front of* MRS HOPKINS, SALLY *is watching from the doorway.*

MRS HOPKINS: Dave won't be working here any more.
> JOE *is staring at the massive clump of keys.*

MRS HOPKINS: We want to offer his job to you, Joe, except at night of course. We have arranged for a proper security guard to come here at night. So – how do you feel about that? The job?

JOE: Good. That's fine. (*Then, suddenly.*) He didn't jump, did he? Dave? Off the roof?!

MRS HOPKINS (*very startled*): No, of course not. What gave you that idea?! He's gone back to Scotland, he was missing home.

JOE: That's lucky . . . that he didn't jump!
> MRS HOPKINS *looks baffled.*

MRS HOPKINS: So, Joe, you'll be here all day until Mr James, the security guard, arrives at night. That will mean between 6 p.m. and 9 p.m. you will be alone in the house. (*Firmly.*) And during that time you mustn't let anybody in. *Nobody.* Don't answer the door. You're just here in case anybody's left a tap running, that sort of thing.
> JOE *is staring fascinated at the large bunch of keys, the sheer variety: the big heavy ones, the small delicate ones.*

MRS HOPKINS: We'll do all the keys tomorrow! And there will be a room here for you, so you can sleep the night here – if you're ever too tired to go home. I'll think you'll find the pay will be very reasonable. We'll do all that tomorrow too.

SALLY: Isn't it marvellous, Joe? Isn't it great? A full-time job, here!

JOE *is calm.*

JOE: Yeah . . . (*He moves, assuming the meeting is over.*) Yeah.

MRS HOPKINS: Joe?

JOE *turns.*

MRS HOPKINS: You're sure you won't be nervous being in the house on your own?

JOE *seems surprised at the question. He smiles.*

JOE: Don't think so . . .

INT. HALL. EVENING

High shot of the empty marble hall, loud rock music playing from somewhere in the house. JOE *suddenly runs into shot, whooping euphorically and really loudly. He is holding the bunch of keys. He hurtles up the grand staircase, shouting excitedly.*

We cut to him standing in an empty reception room surrounded by stacked banqueting chairs. He swings round holding the keys, the music loud from his stereo.

A great big smile on JOE's *face, thrilled to be alone in the big house.*

We cut to him sitting in the kitchen with his feet up. A nice mug of tea in front of him, he is eating a large currant bun and counting the keys on the key ring.

He suddenly becomes aware a voice is calling from outside: 'Mr Joe . . . Mr Joe!'

He looks out of the window. At number 36 across the road, a young Filipino woman is standing on the doorstep calling for him.

EXT. CENTRAL LONDON STREET. EVENING

JOE *crosses the street, his solid rolling walk. A subjective shot as he approaches the door of Number 36. The* MAID *is gesturing to him.*

MAID: He wants some meats . . . (JOE *looks blank.*) Mr
    Graham wants some cooked meats . . . you choose at
    the shop – the deli . . . (*She points round the corner.*)
    You just sign – (*mimes a big signature in the air*) and
    show this . . . (*gives* JOE *a plain red card, not a credit
    card, just simple red plastic*) for the meats . . .

INT. THE DELICATESSEN. EVENING
*The dark interior of the Italian delicatessen, full of pungent
sights. The window is so festooned with cheeses, Italian cakes
and cooked meats that the evening sunlight is almost entirely
shut out and the shop becomes a shadowy Aladdin's cave of
food.*

*There is a rather sour-faced elderly Italian woman in the
shadows behind the counter, a younger Italian man who is
reading a newspaper and an Englishwoman,* TINA, *in her late
twenties.* JOE *stares at them: they are framed by all the food.*

TINA: Can I help you?
JOE: Come to choose Mr Graham's cooked meats . . .
TINA: New, are you? Dave used to do that.
    JOE *holds up the plain red card.* TINA *smiles.*
TINA: The red card! Not the greatest bit of ID ever, is it?!
    JOE *is pressing his face up to the glass of the counter,
    staring at all the salamis and cheeses.*
TINA: Mr Graham usually has about three hundred grams
    of Milano and some –
JOE: I'll have some of that – (*pointing at a more exotic-
    looking salami with hazelnuts*) and then some of that –
    (*points to a fine ham*) and some of this too!
TINA: Wow! This is a new regime! How many grams do
    you want of each?
JOE: Oh, I think seven hundred and fifty each . . .
TINA: What?!

JOE: OK – make it a thousand then. A round thousand of
each. (*He presses his face right up against the glass,
pointing to some Parma ham.*) And we'll have some of
that too, just in case.

INT. NUMBER 36. ELLIOT'S HOUSE. EVENING
We cut to two Filipino MAIDS *and* JOE, *each carrying a large
tray towards the camera. The trays are groaning under the
weight of slices of salami, now carefully arranged on fine china.*

They enter the reception room in ELLIOT's *house. It is on a
much smaller scale than the great house across the road. Much
more domestic.*

ELLIOT *is standing in the centre of the room, fidgeting
slightly. He smiles a shy smile.*

ELLIOT: Most kind . . . that's most kind.
As the MAIDS *arrange the plates of cooked meats on a
table near the window,* JOE *stares at the walls of the room.
Most of the decor is comfortable, slightly old-fashioned and
unremarkable. But in among the conventional there are
a few unusual features. A couple of collages which create
human forms are displayed on the walls: one seems to be of
a very old man bent double, and the other a figure standing
staring out, his face made up of different bits of coloured
photos that have been cut out of magazines.*

The face is very disquieting.

*There is also a cabinet displaying some oriental knives
and daggers, one or two of which look particularly lethal.*
ELLIOT (*staring at the salami*): My word! What a selection!
Thanks, Joe.
JOE *puts the red plastic card down on the table.*
ELLIOT: Keep that . . .
The MAIDS *are withdrawing.* JOE *turns to follow.*
ELLIOT: Where are you going?

JOE: Got to get back to the other house . . .

ELLIOT smiles. His manner polite, almost humble.

ELLIOT: I would appreciate it . . . if you would stay for a moment.

JOE stares at the knives out of the corner of his eye.

JOE: Not sure I can. I am not meant to leave the house, sir.

ELLIOT: It'll be fine. (*Smiles.*) I'll explain to Mrs Hopkins. (ELLIOT *approaches the cooked meats.*) You've done a really terrific job here, Joe, some of these I don't think I've ever tasted before.

JOE: Good . . . sir.

ELLIOT: Absolutely. It is good. No need to call me sir. (*He smiles.*) You really mustn't call me sir.

JOE: Right.

There is a pause. The strange collage of pictures peers at JOE *from the wall.*

ELLIOT: I can't possibly gobble all this myself . . . (*He looks at* JOE.) You wouldn't, would you – ? (ELLIOT *is facing* JOE *with the frightening pictures behind him.*) Like some too . . . ?

JOE hesitates for a moment.

JOE: Sure . . .

Time cut. ELLIOT *and* JOE *are at opposite ends of the table, silently munching through the cooked meats. For a moment they just eat, helping themselves to different pieces of salami and ham. There is bread on the table, but neither of them is eating it.*

JOE glances up from his salami selection to stare at the unsettling collages, especially the figure that is staring out. He sees now that the figure is dressed in battle fatigues.

ELLIOT *follows* JOE*'s gaze.*

ELLIOT: Funny, aren't they . . . ? (*He smiles.*) A bit odd, maybe? They are meant to be me, actually! . . . I did them last summer. That one – (*he points to the old bent*

figure) that's showing me near the end . . . and the
other is . . . (*he smiles*) well, just me . . . !
JOE *stares at the strange figure.*
ELLIOT: I was brought up all over the world . . .
JOE *sees the pictures come from many countries.*
ELLIOT: My father owned a lot of hotels. (*He smiles.*) Among
other things . . . (*He chuckles, a self-deprecating chuckle.*)
Maybe it makes me look a little too cheerful . . . !
JOE *stares at the collage: the haunting, disquieting, mottled
face.*

INT./EXT. HALL/STREET. LATE AFTERNOON
We cut to JOE *in different clothes. It is another evening. He is
sitting at his desk, which is now adorned by a vase of flowers
and a few other accessories: a large rubber, a stapler and a box
of drawing pins.* JOE *is listening to his Discman.*
There is a knock at the front door, heard through the music.
JOE *takes off his headphones. He hears the knock again, a sharp,
incisive knock.*
We cut to JOE *sliding open the panel.* RICHARD *is standing
there in the late-afternoon sun. As soon as* RICHARD *sees* JOE
he greets him with a warm charming smile.

RICHARD: It's you again! Hi! (*A very slight pause.*) Is Dave
there?
JOE: Dave's left. Doesn't work here any more.
RICHARD: Right . . . Well, maybe you could help me? I just
wanted to show a friend of mine this place.
JOE: No.
RICHARD (*smiles*): You sure?
JOE: I can't open this door after six o'clock to anyone.
At the very moment JOE *is saying this, a young woman
steps next to* RICHARD. *She has been waiting just outside*
JOE*'s field of vision. But now through the panel* JOE *sees*

this beautiful face – a woman in her late twenties or early thirties. She is exquisitely dressed.

RICHARD (*breezy smile*): This is Charlotte . . . this is Joe.

CHARLOTTE: Hi, Joe.

JOE *nods to her through the panel.*

RICHARD: So – you can't open it to anyone? Even for Charlotte here?

JOE: No. (*Staring at* CHARLOTTE.) Except . . .

RICHARD: Except?

JOE: Except if I know the person that's asking . . .

INT. HALL. LATE AFTERNOON

CHARLOTTE *and* RICHARD *step inside the hall.* CHARLOTTE *swings round, taking in the place, which is splashed with late-evening sun.*

CHARLOTTE: Wow! It's magnificent! And so beautifully kept . . . (*She moves, touching the banister.*) Like it's waiting for something . . .

RICHARD (*smiles*): That's right (*He moves.*) That's what you can do when you're worth four billion – keep something in perfect condition and totally empty!

CHARLOTTE (*turns to* JOE): It's a palace . . . ! And you've got it all to yourself, Joe . . . ? That's exciting, that's fabulous . . . !

JOE: Only after six, I've got it to myself after six. And the security guard comes at nine. But I stay here at my desk mostly, anyway.

RICHARD: Of course. (*Picking up the big bunch of keys.*) But you should explore, shouldn't you? While you've got the chance, see what these keys unlock! . . . You should go into every single room in the place, count them. JOE *takes back the keys.*

JOE: Yeah . . . I will . . . I'll do that.

RICHARD: And have they given you your own room, Joe?

JOE (*smiles*): Yeah. They have! Do you want to see it?

We cut to them entering JOE's *little room on the ground floor. There is a single bed and a sink. The window looks out over the courtyard with its flowering shrubs and pond.*

On the wall there is the big black-and-white photograph of the wombat, from his room in south London.

RICHARD: I like your room very much. That's a wombat, isn't it? I always wanted a wombat.

JOE (*staring at the picture*): He's good, isn't he?! I sleep here about once a week, when I can't be bothered to go home.

RICHARD's *mobile rings, he checks the number and then switches the phone off.*

JOE *sees* RICHARD's *fingers touch* CHARLOTTE's, *entwine round them. Their hands touch for a moment and then part.*

RICHARD (*smiling at* JOE): Great! Can I show Charlotte upstairs, Joe?

JOE *hesitates.*

JOE: I should stay at the desk . . . even though I don't let anyone in – but I check them out. So I like to stay round the desk.

RICHARD: That's OK! I know the way! I'll show Charlotte.

We cut to JOE *sitting at the desk. We can hear their voices and laughter ringing round the house upstairs, but he can't hear what they are saying.*

We cut to RICHARD *and* CHARLOTTE *by the door of one of the bedrooms upstairs. The passage tapers away behind them into shadow.*

CHARLOTTE: It's amazing, this place . . . with only the boy here – that's so . . . (*she smiles*) unexpected.

RICHARD: I know!

CHARLOTTE: But it seems so right . . . in a way too . . . for this building. (*She stares down the passage, which looks mysterious in the evening light.*) For a secret place like this.

RICHARD: So, what about it?! I'll ask Elliot, shall I? I know him – I can ask him!

CHARLOTTE (*laughing*): You wouldn't dare! Even you wouldn't dare do that!

RICHARD (*laughs, touching her*): Maybe you're right . . . !
We cut to CHARLOTTE *and* RICHARD *coming down the stairs, staring down at* JOE *who is sitting at his desk with all his keys.*

RICHARD (*calling down at him*): You look great at your desk! Really official now!

CHARLOTTE: Thanks, Joe . . . for letting us see that. It's a beautiful house.

RICHARD: It is.
RICHARD *moves with* CHARLOTTE *to the door.*

JOE: Are you seeing Mr Graham today?

RICHARD: No, not today.
RICHARD *suddenly turns on an impulse and approaches* JOE.

RICHARD: But if you see him, or rather when you next see him, could you ask him something, Joe? For me?
CHARLOTTE *is standing across the hall in her beautiful dress. She is smiling, shaking her head, almost laughing at* RICHARD's *audacity.*

JOE: Yes? What?

RICHARD (*quietly*): Ask if Charlotte and I can come and visit this place again . . . at this sort of time, when you're in charge. And maybe visit one of the rooms upstairs.

JOE: One of the rooms upstairs?

RICHARD: Yes, use one of those rooms as a place to rest after a busy day . . . (*He smiles straight at* JOE, *as if they are both men of the world.*) A little oasis, just for a couple of hours . . . (*Smiles.*) He will understand . . .

JOE: Right . . .

> JOE *looks across at* CHARLOTTE. *She is laughing silently and shaking her head. When she sees* JOE *watching her, she smiles at him.*

RICHARD: There's no hurry. Ask him whenever you like . . . when the chance comes up. (*He smiles.*) Because I know you're not meant to let anyone in.

> RICHARD *moves back towards* CHARLOTTE, *who waves to* JOE. *They seem full of energy and life.*

CHARLOTTE: Thank you, Joe.

RICHARD (*pointing at the keys*): And don't forget to go exploring for me!

EXT./INT. ROOFTOPS. AFTERNOON
We see a large Maine Coon cat, a fine, long-haired specimen with tufted ears, walking along the roof of the house among the chimneys. We then cut to the courtyard garden and see the same cat jumping down into the garden. We then see it peering through the window into the main marble hall where all the cleaners are polishing and JOE *is sitting at his desk.* JOE *glances up and exchanges looks with the cat. We hear a church clock beginning to strike six.*

INT. HALL, PASSAGES AND ROOMS. LATE AFTERNOON
We see the cleaners all leaving. MRS HOPKINS *turns in the doorway. She sees* JOE *has already moved away from his desk and is standing rattling his keys, quietly excited.*

MRS HOPKINS: All right, Joe?

JOE: Oh yes!

> *As soon as* MRS HOPKINS *has gone,* JOE *moves off with great purpose through the house.*

A series of strong cuts, forming a rapid montage of JOE
*exploring the building and using all his keys. We see him
unlock a number of doors to reveal different interiors. An
empty ballroom with just two huge chandeliers and one
small table with a vase of orange flowers on it; a very large
wine cellar; a room full of junk, some of which is nearly a
hundred years old.* JOE *moves further along the basement.
He unlocks a red door and finds himself staring at a small
jewel-like private cinema with plaster decorations.*

*He moves to another door in the basement and is about
to unlock it when he sees it is already fractionally open.*

*He pushes it wide open and then leaps back with an
involuntary scream. Standing immediately behind the door
as it swings open is* ELLIOT.

JOE *is incredibly shocked to see him standing there in
the half-shadow.*

Behind ELLIOT *are lines and lines of boxes with paper
sticking out of them.*

ELLIOT (*smiles*): No need to scream when you see me.

JOE: I wasn't . . . I didn't mean . . .

He stares at ELLIOT, *who is covered in dust.*

JOE: I didn't know you were in the house, Mr Graham.

ELLIOT: I was just going though some boxes. Something
that needs to be done . . .

JOE: Yes . . .

ELLIOT *begins to move away along the basement passage.*

ELLIOT: I'll just have a little wash and brush-up. (*He
stops.*) Then maybe . . . ? Can I ? . . . Can I take you
for a meal? (*Staring straight at* JOE.) It would be great
if you could come.

JOE *hesitates.*

JOE (*quiet*): OK . . .

INT. RESTAURANT. NIGHT

We cut inside the dark interior of an oriental restaurant specialising in fish. There is a tank full of lobsters lit by a blue light. The interior is exceptionally gloomy with waiters looming out of the shadows.

The other diners are just shapes in the sepulchral atmosphere.

JOE: I'll have the lobster. (*He points at the tank.*) A couple of those lobsters, please.

The waiter shows a flick of surprise at two lobsters, but writes down the order.

ELLIOT: I think I'll have the sea bass . . . Yes, I think that's right . . . No, wait – I think maybe the turbot, I'll go for the turbot . . .

The waiter begins to write this down.

No, wait . . . the giant tiger prawn, maybe that's a better idea . . . ? (*He looks up, genuinely undecided.*) No, I think the turbot with ginger . . . I'll go with that . . . I think . . . Yes, I think so –

The waiter stares at him for a second, then writes it down and leaves. ELLIOT, his face half in shadow, looks across at JOE.

ELLIOT (*smiles*): All that money – and he still can't decide!

JOE is watching him carefully.

ELLIOT: If that's what you were thinking, Joe, you'd be right . . .

We see the impassive faces of the waiters staring out of the shadows.

It's not the friendliest place here – but I like that, no chit-chat! When I go out, and I do go out – I hate the idea of being a recluse – people can often be quite strange, you know . . . how they react around me . . .

JOE looking at ELLIOT's face in the blue light. ELLIOT is looking very thoughtful. We stay on his face.

ELLIOT: Yes . . . people are either very loud and talkative –

like they've taken a bet with somebody before coming
up to me . . .

INT. PARTY/RESTAURANT. NIGHT
*We cut to a room full of coloured lights and gentle party music.
We see a* WOMAN *pushing her face close to* ELLIOT; *she is
holding her champagne glass and seems quite drunk.*

PARTY WOMAN: Write a cheque, can't you, for a couple
of million before the end of the night! FOR ME! (*She
laughs.*) Just go for it . . . it'll make us both feel so
good . . . !
We cut back to ELLIOT *in the gloom of the fish restaurant.*
ELLIOT: Or else, you know, they're embarrassed – don't
want anybody to think they might be after something
if they talk to me, that they might be looking for
donations . . . so they just –
We cut back to the room full of coloured lights. We see
ELLIOT *drinking on his own as a huddle of people stand
with their backs to him, ostentatiously talking amongst
themselves.*
We cut back to ELLIOT.
ELLIOT: Or they go on and on about the most unlikely
subjects . . .
*We cut back to the party room. A man has pushed himself
really close to* ELLIOT *and is talking in a confidential
tone.*
INVENTOR: I've got something that I think will really
interest you – I've invented a new sort of toilet brush,
that cleans itself after it's cleaned the toilet.
We cut back to ELLIOT. *He smiles his self-deprecating
smile.*
ELLIOT: Yes, it can be strange . . . (*A shadow passes across*
ELLIOT's *face, as if he is experiencing a twinge of pain.*

The shadow passes. He looks across at JOE.) And what
about you, Joe?

JOE: Me . . . ? I've left school.

ELLIOT: And?

JOE: That's all.

ELLIOT *is staring at him; he looks alarming in the blue
light.*

ELLIOT: And you don't get frightened when you're all
alone in the house?

JOE: I'm not frightened of the house!

ELLIOT: Right . . . What are you frightened of?

ELLIOT *studies* JOE's *face.* JOE *is trying hard not to show
he's slightly scared of him.*

JOE: I'll have to think . . . you know . . . what I'm scared
of –

The food arrives just in time, stopping JOE *having to say
any more.* JOE's *huge plate of double lobster is placed in
front of him. He immediately starts trying to crack one of
the claws.*

ELLIOT: That looks good.

JOE *nods, as he sets about the lobster.*

ELLIOT: So, Joe, if I was to ask you to take a few messages
for me, you wouldn't mind? To be a messenger for
me? Just once or twice?

JOE (*pulling at the lobster*): I wouldn't mind, no . . . That
would be all right . . . (*He suddenly stops eating, and
looks at* ELLIOT.) I have a message for you. I've got
one already – just remembered!

ELLIOT: Which is?

JOE: From a man called Richard Reece –

ELLIOT: Ah yes, Richard!

JOE: He wants to know if he can use the house between six
and nine, use a room, an upstairs room . . . he and
a friend, she's called Charlotte . . . as a place to rest
after a busy day . . .

ELLIOT: He does, does he?! (*He chuckles to himself.*) Do
you know who he is?

JOE: Yeah . . . he's a member of the government –

ELLIOT: Yes, he is the youngest member of the Cabinet
and a very bright guy. Really smart! But he is married
and his constituency is in London . . . so he doesn't
have a separate flat . . . you know, away from his
family . . . (*He chuckles to himself.*) I can see it would
be perfect . . . He can tell everyone he is visiting me!
(*He smiles to himself.*) What's the woman like?

JOE: She's OK . . . (*Eating lobster.*) She's quite pretty.
ELLIOT *looks interested.* JOE *munches.*

JOE: Really pretty . . .

ELLIOT: Well, that's an intriguing message, Joe. (*He smiles
to himself.*) It might be good for something to happen
in that house . . . We'll see . . . (*He watches* JOE *eating
the lobster.*) So, Joe – are you reliable? To take the
messages? Can you be relied on?

JOE *doesn't look up, continues to concentrate on his food.*

ELLIOT: Did you hear what I said, Joe?

JOE *looks up.* ELLIOT *is staring straight at him. Again, in
the dark restaurant he looks quite scary.*

JOE: Yes . . . I think so. I think I can . . .

INT. PASSAGE AND MEETING ROOM. DAY
We are tracking with JOE *down a passage leading to a meeting
room in an office block. As* JOE *moves towards the door in the
meeting room we hear his voice-over.*

JOE (*voice-over*): So in the last few days I've begun to take
messages for him . . . It usually happens in the
afternoons and I have to take a letter . . . like to these
guys that run all his money . . . take care of it.

We see JOE *go through the door into the meeting room
where there are about eight people in business suits sitting
around a long table. At the head is the accountant,*
FOSTER. *They all look up as* JOE *comes in.*

JOE: Mr Graham won't be coming along today. I got an
envelope here . . . which he said would make everything
clear.

FOSTER: Right (*Patronising smile.*) Well, I think we know
how to keep things ticking over until we next see Mr
Graham . . .

JOE is already leaving.

FOSTER: Do we know when that's going to be?

JOE (*in doorway*): Mr Graham said everything is in the
envelope.

INT. SMALL VICTORIAN HOUSE. DAY

JOE (*voice-over*): And then there was another one, I think
it was on Tuesday, when the person seemed a bit
upset . . .

We see JOE *entering a small sitting room in a Victorian
house. The room is very white. A figure in dark clothes,
a woman in her fifties, is sitting smoking by the window
with her back to the door.*

She doesn't turn round when JOE *enters.*

JOE: Mr Graham says he can't have dinner tonight after
all.

The woman blows a cloud of cigarette smoke.

DARK LADY: Is that what he says . . . ? I doubt that he can
remember what I look like . . . (*She turns and looks at*
JOE.) Maybe that's a good thing . . . !

A look of slight desperation in the woman's eyes. JOE *hands
her the envelope.*

JOE: He said it's all in the envelope . . .

The WOMAN *looks at him sadly.*

EXT./INT. MODERN GOVERNMENT OFFICES. DAY
*JOE is standing on the pavement outside a big government
building. It is raining, he is holding an umbrella. His face is
pressed right up to the glass, staring into the foyer.*

JOE (*voice-over*): And yesterday I took the important
message, the one Mr Reece had asked me about . . .
We cut inside the foyer. RICHARD *is moving across it with
his entourage of advisers. He sees* JOE*'s face pressed up
against the glass.*

RICHARD (*to the security guards*): Let the boy in, I know
him . . .
*JOE comes plodding across the foyer towards them in his
clumpy trainers and old T-shirt. Despite the umbrella, he is
very wet and dishevelled.* RICHARD *introduces* JOE *to his
advisers.*

RICHARD: This is Joe, he works with Elliot Graham. As you
know, I meet Mr Graham quite a lot . . . to discuss
the possibility of him contributing to various charities
and projects in my constituency . . . Just give us a
moment together. (*To* JOE.) Come and sit over here –
We stay with the advisers as they watch RICHARD *sit with*
JOE *in the corner of the foyer.* JOE *swings his legs casually.
He looks very incongruous in the impersonal modern
foyer.*
We cut close to RICHARD *and* JOE.

RICHARD: I'm sorry they didn't let you in, Joe. It's very
good to see you.

JOE: Yeah. I've got a reply to your message. He says it's
OK. Mr Graham. He said he wants the house to be
used for something.

RICHARD: Is that what he said? (*He smiles.*) Well, that's
good, isn't it . . . ?! (*He indicates his entourage waiting
across the foyer.*) See all of those? . . . They are my
advisers. We're going off for an awayday to discuss

strategies and targets and systems and that sort of thing . . . (*Playful smile.*) An awayday where we won't have one new thought between us . . . (*He leans towards* JOE.) Let them wait a moment, it's good for them to see something that doesn't quite fit. You and me talking. (*He grins.*) Not the usual sort of adviser!

INT. THE DELICATESSEN. EVENING
We cut to an array of crumbling blue cheeses. Large whole organic cheeses, including giant farmhouse Cheddars covered in a very deep mould.
   We cut wide to see JOE *flicking the red plastic down on the counter in the delicatessen and inspecting the cheeses.* TINA *is watching him.*

JOE: I like that colour.
TINA: That one?
JOE: The one that is really, really mouldy.
TINA: Is that what he is into now, old cheeses?! When you're worth a few billion but all you want to make you happy is some blue cheese?! Is that it? Is that what he's like?
   JOE *has picked up a handful of Italian amaretti sweets for himself.*
JOE: I don't know . . . I'm only the messenger.

INT. ELLIOT'S HOUSE. RECEPTION ROOM. DUSK
The cheeses are spread out on the table in ELLIOT*'s house.* JOE *is standing in the doorway of the reception room,* ELLIOT *is on the other side of the room.*

ELLIOT: They're a wonderful colour. The cheeses. You've bought a great selection Joe.

JOE: Good.

> JOE *sees out of the corner of his eye that the cabinet with the knives is open.*

ELLIOT: You don't want to stay and help me eat them?

JOE: Can't tonight . . . got to get back.

ELLIOT: Right. (*He smiles.*) Fine. Just before you go I want to show you something . . .

INT. ELLIOT'S HOUSE. NARROW ROOM. DUSK
We cut to a bare light bulb coming on in a long narrow room. The shutters are closed on all the windows. The room is crammed with boxes and bundles of paper, packed tight together. ELLIOT *beckons to* JOE, *who is hanging back in the passage.*

ELLIOT: Come on . . . come in here. It's all right, there's nothing alarming in here. (*Self-deprecating chuckle.*) Unless you count me, of course . . .

> JOE *moves into the narrow room. The walls are covered in drawings and photos of the large house. Some photos of it as it used to be at the beginning of the twentieth century, grand and opulent, and then as it was just after the Second World War, shabby and with blackened walls. And there are also drawings of the house, impressionistic, fantastical pictures showing it as a dark, forbidding place.*

ELLIOT: Thought you would like to see these pictures of the big house . . . as it used to be . . . and some drawings I did of it . . .

> JOE *stares at the disturbing drawings.*

ELLIOT: Not sure what I am saying in them – maybe that I found the house very spooky when I was a child, which I did . . .

> JOE *shrugs.*

JOE: Spooky?

Elliot staring across at the big house.

Joe meets Richard for the first time.

Tina and Joe in the deli.

Joe takes the little animals to the *Antiques Roadshow*.

Elliot addresses the seven richest men in Britain.

oe exploring the big house.

Charlotte during her affair with Richard.

Richard and Charlotte.

Elliot and Joe waiting to find out what Tina has discovered.

Elliot and Joe together at the castle.

Elliot's father with his Nazi colleagues. 'They certainly do things differently here.'

Elliot, Joe and Tina sharing food from the deli at the end of the film.

ELLIOT: And which you clearly do not . . . ! I'm trying
to find out a lot more about the house, both before
and after my father bought it . . . Old houses decay
amazingly quickly when they're empty, so that's why
I am keeping this one alive until I've found out more
and decided what to do with it . . . (*He smiles at* JOE.)
So maybe it's not as barmy as it seems?!
JOE looks at him, not sure what he means.

ELLIOT: Having it cleaned all the time . . .
There is also a picture of a medieval castle with a moat.
JOE stares, fascinated, at the castle.

JOE: The castle is nice.

ELLIOT: Ah yes . . . it is, isn't it! I'll tell you about the
castle one day.
*JOE is staring at the photo of a very beautiful woman in
a fifties dress.*

ELLIOT: You like her? She is my mother.
JOE pushes his face close to the picture.

JOE: She's pretty.

ELLIOT: She was very beautiful. She was much younger
than my father. He married very late. He was rather
a distant sort of guy, Joe! (*Looking at a photo of his
mother.*) She died when I was six . . . I only have a
very few memories of her. I wish I had more . . . ! (*He
smiles.*) Her bending over me . . . smelling gorgeous –
that sort of thing . . .
We move in on the photo of the beautiful woman as JOE
stares at her, fascinated.

EXT./INT. FRONT DOOR/HALL OF THE LARGE HOUSE.
EARLY EVENING
We cut to the front door opening. CHARLOTTE *is standing there
looking glamorous. She is again beautifully and fashionably
dressed.* JOE *smiles at her and she gives him a warm smile back.*

CHARLOTTE: Hello, Joe. How are you?

JOE: I'm fine.

> CHARLOTTE *enters the hall. For a moment* JOE *looks at her across the marble floor.*

JOE: Can I get you something?

CHARLOTTE: Thank you. Maybe a glass of water . . .

INT. KITCHEN. EARLY EVENING

The cold tap is running. CHARLOTTE *is leaning against the pots in the kitchen.*

JOE: I'm just letting it run so it's really nice and cold.

CHARLOTTE: Thank you, Joe. (*She sees a little cluster of the amaretti sweets.*) Can I have one of these?

JOE: Sure . . . (*He smiles.*) Take as many as you like.

CHARLOTTE: Then I'll take two . . . (*She smiles.*) One for later . . .

> *There is a sharp knock at the front door.*

JOE: There he is! (*He heads off.*) I'll let him in.

> *We stay on* CHARLOTTE. *She is moving among all the old pots and jars in the kitchen and piles of forty-year-old colour supplements.* RICHARD *appears in the depth of field and calls across to the kitchen.*

RICHARD: Here we all are!

> *We move with* CHARLOTTE *as she enters the hall.*
> RICHARD *watches her approach.*

RICHARD: You look great. (*He turns to* JOE *with a smile.*) Doesn't she look great?!

> JOE *nods, watching them both.*

RICHARD: Joe . . . we'll just go upstairs for a little while . . . as arranged. And you'll be all right down here? At your desk?

> JOE *is standing by his desk.*

JOE: Yeah . . . of course.

CHARLOTTE *and* RICHARD *start to climb the stairs.* JOE *is leaning on the desk, writing something.*

JOE: Just wait! Wait a minute –

CHARLOTTE *and* RICHARD *stop in surprise.* JOE *hands them a piece of paper.*

JOE: Just call me on my mobile if you need anything.

RICHARD: Thank you, Joe . . . great.

We cut to CHARLOTTE *and* RICHARD *moving along the upstairs passage,* CHARLOTTE *glancing at the bedrooms as they pass, pushing open the doors.*

RICHARD: I've already chosen one . . . (*He smiles.*) I think you'll approve . . .

CHARLOTTE: Maybe we should give Joe some money so he can go to the movies or something – it's a little bit weird, isn't it, him being downstairs?!

RICHARD (*smiles*): No weirder then going to a hotel and a lot more private then going to a friend's flat . . . ! (*Softly, touching* CHARLOTTE.) He'd be upset if we asked him to go out– he's the concierge.

RICHARD *pushes open the door of a bedroom with beautiful wallpaper of tropical birds. It gives the room a Chinese feel.*

CHARLOTTE: Wow – that's lovely! What a fantastic room!

RICHARD (*starting to kiss her neck*): I'm glad you like it –

They start to kiss passionately against the wall.

CHARLOTTE (*suddenly stops*): What about Elliot Graham?

RICHARD: What about him? He's not going to pop up! (*He smiles.*) He wants the house to be used . . .

INT. HALL/BEDROOM. EVENING

We cut down to JOE *arranging his pencils carefully on his desk.*

We cut back to CHARLOTTE *and* RICHARD *shedding their clothes.* RICHARD *taking* CHARLOTTE'S *bra off,* CHARLOTTE *his shirt.*

CHARLOTTE: Does the door lock?

RICHARD: I've locked it.

> CHARLOTTE's *head goes back as he kisses her naked shoulders. She's excited, full of desire, but she keeps stopping* RICHARD.

CHARLOTTE: Joe won't hear anything?

RICHARD (*kissing her very sexually*): In a house this size, no chance!

> CHARLOTTE *half stops him again, though they are still kissing, small kisses.*

CHARLOTTE: Joe's not going to come rushing upstairs? All excited, is he?

RICHARD (*smiles*): Probably not . . . we'll find out . . .

> *We cut to a track towards* JOE *sitting at his desk listening to his Discman. The track starts far away from him so we see him as a small figure in the big hall.*
>
> *We intercut the track with* CHARLOTTE *and* RICHARD *naked in bed making passionate love. As the camera closes in on* JOE, *we see his face impassive, seemingly lost in the music.*
>
> *We cut back to a close up of* CHARLOTTE, *her head thrown back as she moans loudly.*
>
> *We cut back to* JOE. *He takes his headphones off slowly. There is total silence in the hall.* JOE *carefully and methodically changes the CD.*
>
> *We cut back to* CHARLOTTE *and* RICHARD *as they climax loudly, surrounded by all the tropical birds.*

INT. HALL/BEDROOM. EVENING

We cut to JOE's *mobile phone ringing. He picks it up, adopting a rather formal tone as if he is on reception.*

JOE: Yes?

RICHARD (*voice-over*): Are you all right, Joe?

JOE: Yes. I am fine . . . Do you want anything?

RICHARD (*voice-over*): That's very kind, but no . . . we'll be down in a moment.

We cut to CHARLOTTE *and* RICHARD *lying naked in the bed, as* RICHARD *rings off.*

RICHARD: He asked if we wanted anything.

CHARLOTTE *smiles at this. She is staring at the wallpaper of the birds.*

CHARLOTTE: I wonder when this room was last used . . .

INT. HALL. DUSK

We cut to RICHARD *coming down the staircase. He looks immaculate as if he has just been chairing a meeting.*

RICHARD: Thank you, Joe. I'm off now.

JOE *watches him go. His voice-over starts.*

JOE (*voice-over*): He leaves first . . . and then she stays for a bit and leaves about fifteen minutes later.

We see CHARLOTTE *smiling at* JOE *at the bottom of the stairs.*

JOE (*voice-over*): Sometimes we have a little chat together . . .

INT. KITCHEN/HALLWAY. DAY

We see JOE *sitting writing in his book, the ledger.*

JOE (*voice-over*): I've decided to write it down, because nobody is reading this book, and I want to remember it. *He looks up and we see a shot of* CHARLOTTE *sitting on the stairs in the hallway looking down at* JOE *and smiling.* They always phone in the morning to tell me to expect them. The whole day changes when I know they are going to visit! They visited three times last week – which made it a really good week.

We see the panel slide back in the front door and
CHARLOTTE *is standing there.*

JOE (*voice-over*): She looks really amazing each time – her
hair was different yesterday . . . He always arrives
separately . . .

We see RICHARD *moving up the stairs, waving at* JOE.
We see JOE *sitting at his desk with his feet up.*

JOE (*voice-over*): I think they've stopped worrying about me
going upstairs . . .

We move in on JOE*'s eyes.*

INT. BEDROOM. EVENING
We cut to RICHARD *and* CHARLOTTE *making love. We cut
back to a close-up of* JOE *thinking about them and then*
RICHARD *and* CHARLOTTE *entwined together, making love.*

JOE (*voice-over*): Which of course I would never do.

INT. BASEMENT. UTILITY ROOM. NIGHT
We cut to JOE *in front of two huge old washing machines which are clanking loudly.*

JOE (*voice-over*): I do the sheets . . . because I don't know what Mrs Hopkins will say . . . and I think it's probably best that she doesn't know . . .

INT. BEDROOM. DAY
We cut to JOE *carefully making the bed, putting new linen on and arranging everything carefully.*

JOE (*voice-over*): I don't know if they wonder how they get clean sheets all the time . . . Not sure they ever wonder about it, really!
We see JOE *smoothing the corners of the bed.*

INT. KITCHEN. EVENING
We see RICHARD *making himself a peanut butter sandwich in the kitchen.*

JOE (*voice-over*): Mr Reece spends time with me sometimes . . . on his way out. I like both of them. He is a very clever man.
RICHARD: Peanut butter is the answer to everything!
He gives JOE *a peanut butter sandwich, then sits at the kitchen table eating one himself.*
RICHARD: It's quite funny, Joe, me ending up being pally with a billionaire – because we didn't have much when I was small. My father's a railway signalman – he still does it – enjoys telling me every week how we've totally buggered up the railways! For some reason, Joe, I always believed in myself, I was full of confidence all

the time . . . knew I'd get a scholarship . . . knew I'd get a good job . . . knew I'd get into Parliament. Never felt inferior to anybody. (*He smiles.*) And nor should you, Joe! (*Bites into sandwich.*)

JOE: No . . .

RICHARD: Because you don't miss much, do you?!

EXT. THE CENTRAL LONDON STREET. LATE AFTERNOON
We cut to JOE *running down the street towards the house holding a bag from the delicatessen. He hears a voice calling his name. It is* ELLIOT *standing near number 36.*

ELLIOT: You're in a hurry, young man.

JOE: Yeah . . . I just . . . just got to do something.

ELLIOT (*grins*): Got visitors coming, have you?

   JOE *hesitates.*

ELLIOT: Very discreet – that's good, Joe. Admirable!

   JOE *begins to move off and then suddenly turns.*

JOE: You won't . . . ? (*He stops.*)

ELLIOT: Yes Joe?

JOE: You won't just turn up, you know, suddenly? . . . Like when I found you –

   ELLIOT *smiles.*

JOE: Without telling me?

ELLIOT (*chuckles*): I'll try not to.

INT. HALL/PASSAGES/BEDROOM. LATE AFTERNOON
JOE *is rushing up the stairs and down the passage and into the bedroom. He puts the contents from the bag from the deli, a oad of amaretti sweets, in a bowl beside their bed. Just as he is arranging the sweets the doorbell rings. He puts his last touches to the arrangement of the bedroom and then rushes down.*

   He opens the door to CHARLOTTE.

CHARLOTTE: Hi, Joe. You're out of breath.

JOE: No . . . not really.

INT. KITCHEN. LATE AFTERNOON

JOE *is getting* CHARLOTTE *some cold water. She is by the kitchen window staring out into the street. A woman is parking a gigantic four-by-four.*

CHARLOTTE: Who needs an enormous car like that in the city? Ridiculous woman! (*Light laugh.*) Mind you, it could be me in a couple of years!

Her gaze moves from the woman and she suddenly sees ELLIOT *is standing in his house staring directly at her from across the street. She lets out a cry of surprise and leaps back from the window involuntary, as if she was naked.*

CHARLOTTE: Is that Elliot Graham?! Must be, mustn't it! That man staring?

JOE (*glancing out*): Yeah . . . that's him.

CHARLOTTE: Sorry! It's just . . . I don't like the idea of him watching . . . or seeing me at all really . . .

JOE: It's OK. He won't come in.

We stay on ELLIOT *for a moment.*

INT. ELLIOT'S HOUSE. EVENING

We cut inside ELLIOT*'s reception room. He is still standing at the window, staring across at the house. He turns.*

A young historian, WHITTLE, *is seated at the table with a bulky file of papers. He is in mid-flow.*

WHITTLE: . . . I've done ninety-five per cent of your father's papers now, traced his fortune right back to his first job when he was a young man before the war. I've followed all his travels . . . I've looked into how he made his money, both the financial services sector and all the hotels he owned. I've looked into the history of the house too, and I have to say – I know you wanted me to dig really deep – but it's all above board! There are no nasty surprises, no skeletons.

ELLIOT (*relieved smile*): It's all fine, is it? . . . Shipshape?

WHITTLE (*beaming*): Absolutely!

ELLIOT *stares at the young man searchingly. He then turns away deep in thought.*

He glances at the collage of himself, the mottled face, and then the pictures of all his father's hotels.

We move in on ELLIOT*'s eyes, his troubled look.*

WHITTLE: Everything OK, Mr Graham?

ELLIOT *turns back.*

ELLIOT (*quietly*): If what you tell me is true . . . then it is.

INT. THE BEDROOM WITH TROPICAL BIRDS. EVENING

CHARLOTTE *enters the bedroom, exclaiming in delighted surprise.*

CHARLOTTE: Oh wow! Look at this – Joe has provided us with some sweets!

RICHARD: That's fantastic . . . I told you he'd look after us!

CHARLOTTE, *sitting on the bed, is about to eat a sweet when she suddenly stops.*

CHARLOTTE: I saw Elliot Graham just now, staring over here – made me go cold all over for some reason . . .

RICHARD: He's fine . . . a little peculiar, of course, but show me a normal billionaire . . .

CHARLOTTE: Why is he letting us use the house?

RICHARD: Because he likes me. (*Grins.*) And really rates me!

CHARLOTTE (*laughs*): You always think that's the reason for everything!

They roll on the bed fully clothed, kissing passionately.

EXT./INT. SOUTH LONDON FLAT. DUSK

We cut to JOE *on the balcony of the low-rise flats, staring out across the concrete playgrounds. The group of kids that jeered at him before are kicking a ball in a desultory fashion. One of them yells up at* JOE *and does the Neanderthal noises.* JOE *stares back. He is holding his big bunch of keys; he rattles them confidently in his hand.*

SALLY *joins him on the balcony. She is dressed to go out. She looks younger, happier.*

SALLY: You OK, love?

JOE: Yeah.

SALLY: I'm going out tonight.

JOE: Have a good time.

SALLY (*hesitating*): Joe . . . I've met somebody new . . . and he is going to Spain for a few months to work . . . and he's asked me to go with him . . . Would that be OK?

JOE: Yeah. Of course.

SALLY: Sure?

JOE *nods.*

SALLY: Great . . . I think the change will do me good . . . I'll stop cleaning that house! (*She squeezes his hand.*) I feel I've hardly seen you these last few weeks –

JOE: You see me at the house!

SALLY: Yes. (*Smiles.*) But you're always so busy keeping watch by the door.

JOE: Yeah . . . I like keeping watch.

Intense close-up of JOE.

I like being in that house.

INT. KITCHEN. THE LARGE HOUSE. EVENING

We cut to CHARLOTTE *in the kitchen; her head goes back, she is drinking a long cold drink of water. Then she wipes a drop of water off her lips with the back of her hand.*

JOE (*voice-over*): This has just happened . . . a couple of hours ago. One of the greatest days I've had.

CHARLOTTE: That was good! That was so cold.

JOE *is staring at her. She looks beautiful standing there in the kitchen.*

CHARLOTTE: You got any brothers or sisters, Joe?

JOE: No.

CHARLOTTE: And your dad? Where is your dad?

JOE: Oh, he doesn't live with us. He visits once or twice a year.

FLASHBACK. INT. SOUTH LONDON FLAT. DAY
We cut to a small bald man shuffling around the south London flat, occasionally grunting.

JOE: He grunts. Never says anything. Just grunts.

INT. KITCHEN. EVENING

CHARLOTTE: That's not good. A grunting dad . . .

JOE: It's OK.

CHARLOTTE: What about friends? You got some good mates you hang out with?

JOE (*hesitating for a moment*): One or two. Nobody that special.

CHARLOTTE: You should find somebody special, Joe . . . (*Smiles.*) You could if you put your mind to it –

JOE: Yeah, I know.

CHARLOTTE: I'm sure you could do a lot. All sorts of things.

JOE *is watching her, not really listening to her advice.*

JOE: Are you married?

CHARLOTTE (*slight pause*): Yes. I am, Joe. And I also have

two children, aged six and four, Leo and Rachel.
(*She smiles.*) They're great. My kids. Really great.

JOE: And your husband?

CHARLOTTE: Thought you might ask that! He's great
too . . . he's a lawyer. He works very hard. (*She
smiles.*) He's terrific.

JOE *is watching her.*

CHARLOTTE: No more questions?

JOE: No.

CHARLOTTE: You can ask me, Joe . . . since I know you
won't tell anyone. (*Softly.*) I trust you . . .

She touches his head fondly. Strokes his hair. We stay on
JOE's *eyes, feeling this intensely, her warm touch.*

JOE: I haven't got any more questions . . .

CHARLOTTE: I'm about to go back to work . . . now the
kids are both going to school. I was a lobbyist . . .
I am a lobbyist for my sins, you know, a political
lobbyist – that's how I met Richard. (*Touches his hair
fondly again.*) I'm very lucky, aren't I, Joe?! . . . I'm
very, very lucky.

They stare at each other.

JOE: Yeah. So am I . . . (*He grins.*) I'm quite lucky.

INT. GOVERNMENT CAR. DAY
We cut to JOE *leaning his face very close to the passenger
window in the back of a large car.*

JOE (*voice-over*): Had another really good day today!
Richard gave me a lift, just for ten minutes or so . . .

We cut wide to see him sitting with RICHARD *in a
government car.* RICHARD's *red boxes on the seat between
them.*

RICHARD: These are the famous boxes we Cabinet ministers
are meant to treasure so much. (*Picking one up.*) A bit

cheap and cheerful, aren't they! In the old days
apparently they were made of high-quality leather . . .
smelt beautiful. (*Lifting box up to* JOE's *nose.*) That
smells of nothing does it?!

JOE (*smelling box*): Doesn't smell, no!

RICHARD: What do you think of the government car?

JOE (*looking around*): Thought there'd be wood and things
all around, folding seats . . .

RICHARD: Not any more! Mind you, when you're travelling
with the Prime Minister in convoy with all the
motorcycle escorts – that's fantastic! The first time
you do that! You don't stop for anything, Joe, nothing!
I think that's why all leaders go bonkers after a while –
because their car never stops.

JOE *is very intrigued.* RICHARD *notices his interested face.*

RICHARD: You're a clever kid, Joe, been very good to us.
I hope we can call each other friends.

JOE (*smiling broadly*): Yes! (*Leaning against window.*)
Charlotte? . . . She's special, isn't she? . . . To you?

RICHARD: Really special.

JOE *smiles, thinking about this.*

RICHARD: Is everything all right with Mr Graham, Joe?
He's not asking you to do strange things?

JOE (*surprised by this*): What do you mean?

RICHARD: I don't think he's going to try to seduce you,
I didn't mean that! I don't think young men are his
thing. Not sure anything's his thing! I just meant, is
he asking you to do some rather odd tasks?

JOE: No . . . I just take a few messages for him. Sometimes.

RICHARD: Well, let me know if he starts getting too weird.

JOE (*quietly*): Yeah, I will . . . I haven't seen his really
frightening side yet. But I expect I can handle it.

RICHARD: I am sure you can.

INT. HALLWAY/RECEPTION ROOM. ELLIOT'S HOUSE.
SUNDAY AFTERNOON
JOE *enters the small hall of* ELLIOT*'s house. The Filipino maid
is beckoning to him impatiently.*

MAID: Come on, come on, he's waiting for you . . . !
JOE *enters* ELLIOT*'s reception room. There is a television
playing silently in the corner. It is showing* Antiques
Roadshow.
ELLIOT *smiles when he sees* JOE.

ELLIOT: Joe, there you are. Good!
JOE *suddenly notices there is another person in the room,
the historian* WHITTLE, *sitting in the shadows.*

ELLIOT: This is Mr Whittle. He was just on the point of
leaving.

WHITTLE: I was indeed. Because we've finished! (*He
beams.*) Entirely finished – which is marvellous!

ELLIOT: Mr Whittle is an historian and he's been digging
around in my father's papers – at my request – tracing
the history of all his money . . .

WHITTLE (*in the doorway*): And the most rewarding job it's
been too, fascinating! (*He smiles.*) And of course
completely pleasant. (*He leaves.*)

ELLIOT: Do I believe him . . . ?!
A shadow crosses ELLIOT*'s face. We stay on his eyes.
Then he looks at* JOE *and brightens.*

ELLIOT: You look amazed, Joe, that I actually ever see
anybody else!

JOE: No. I wasn't thinking that . . .

ELLIOT (*lightly*): Yes, you were. Well, I do meet people! As
it happens I've just been asked to have my photograph
taken by a Sunday newspaper . . . a group photo of
rich people, would you believe! (*He smiles.*) We will
see if I manage to do it . . .

JOE *is standing in the middle of the room wondering what*
ELLIOT *wants.*

ELLIOT: So, Joe . . . (*He points to* Antiques Roadshow *on
the TV.*) Do you know this programme?

JOE: No.

ELLIOT: People bring antiques from their home to discover
their history . . . (*He smiles.*) and how much they are
worth, of course! (*He indicates two small, jewelled china
animals with diamonds in their eyes sitting on the
mantelpiece.*) I want you to take those objects there –
those little animals – on the show for me.

JOE: Me?

*He stares at the little animals; he sees they have rubies as
their tear ducts.*

ELLIOT: Yes. Oh, and this as well. (*He takes out a beautiful
golden cigar case out of his pocket.*) They're all from one
of the houses my father owned . . . he had houses
everywhere. This one was in Scotland – they're doing
the show from near there. Are you going to take it for
me, Joe?

JOE *hesitates.*

ELLIOT: What's the matter?

JOE *looks awkward.*

ELLIOT: Wondering why I am asking you of all people?

JOE: Yes . . .

ELLIOT: Because I often believe you should use surprising
people to do things . . . that way you might find out
more. (*He looks at the little animals.*) And I need to
find out more about the animals. Would you mind
doing it, Joe?

INT./EXT. ANTIQUES ROADSHOW. DAY
*We see a great hall full of tables covered in antiques. Various
experts are sitting at smaller tables, with members of the public*

*queuing to show the objects they have brought with them. The
television lights glowing down on the hall. People, from all
backgrounds, milling around holding their antiques, holding
huge plates and vases, tiny china figures, slender pieces of silver,
or manoeuvring big pieces of furniture. There are cables running
everywhere.*

We cut outside, we see JOE *getting out of* ELLIOT*'s Mercedes
carrying the little animals and cigar case in a small shoulder
bag.*

We see JOE *peering at all the cables and then stopping by the
door of the OB truck and watching the production team working
by all the monitor screens. They don't notice* JOE *watching them.*

We then see in a series of strong cuts JOE *moving through the
hall. We see everything through* JOE*'s eyes. A hallucinatory feel
as we see him staring at all these people clutching objects from
the past. We see the experts' eyes flick with interest as soon as
they see the jewelled animals and the cigar case.*

We see JOE*'s animals being selected to be one of the featured
antiques on the programme. We see the faces of the researchers
and assistants gathering and looking at the jewelled animals
and talking to* JOE. *We hear someone say, 'When it's your turn,
just don't look into the cameras . . . Remember, don't look into
the camera.'*

JOE *is watching all the different people in the hall as he
waits. He watches how people are affected by different objects.*

We then see it is his turn to show the antiques to the expert.

EXPERT: This is a spectacular collection of snuffboxes . . .
    can you tell me about them . . . ?
    JOE *looks blank.*
EXPERT: Are they yours?
JOE: No.
EXPERT: Did somebody ask you to bring them here?
JOE: Yeah, my boss.
EXPERT: And do you know how he acquired them?

JOE: No.

The sound is blurring. JOE *keeps looking out of the corner of his eye at the people staring at all these evocative objects, a couple looking jealous, another couple laughing. He sees a woman crying in the corner, her partner moving her away. The woman continues to cry.* JOE *stares, fascinated. He watches, trying to work out what's happening over there – a memory seems to have made her sad. All the time the* EXPERT *is talking.*

EXPERT: Well, let's have a little look at them and try and understand what they are all about.

He launches into his description of the two jewelled animals and the cigar case.

This is a snuffbox made of a hard stone, a conglomerate, which is called a pudding stone and the goldsmiths used it to represent the pelt of the leopard. We can see he has heightened that work by giving it little diamond eyes with ruby tear ducts and ruby nostrils and even the gold tongue moves up and down between these rather vicious-looking diamond-set teeth. To have one of those from the court of Frederick the Great of Prussia would be wonderful, but to have two is truly extraordinary. (*Picking up the gold cigar case.*) And this is made for somebody of very, very high rank in about 1900, and let's look inside, polished red gold gleaming away . . .

More and more people are gathering around the table to watch JOE *and his snuffboxes.*

JOE *is hardly listening to the* EXPERT. *A voice out of shot is saying, 'Don't look at the camera, Joe . . . Please don't look at the camera!'* JOE *suddenly jumps up. Remembering he has another object in his pocket, he fumbles around trying to get it out and produces a magnificent moon moth snuffbox.*

EXPERT: There can't be more!

JOE: Yeah, I got this. I was looking at it in the car on the way up.

EXPERT: My goodness me! Well, that is without doubt the most beautiful enamel gold snuffbox I have ever seen. It is an hallucinogenic moth that the goldsmith has actually bought out of his imagination. The moth and the butterfly are emblems of Psyche, goddess of the soul and all higher emotions. This is obviously a love object given from one person to another.

He gets very enthusiastic about the hallucinogenic moon moth.

Can you remember how much your boss paid for all of these?

JOE: Dunno.

EXPERT: Well, do you know how much they're worth?

JOE: A lot . . . (*slight grin*) more than most china animals . . . you know, that you put money in. (*He indicates one of the animals that looks like a piggy bank.*)

EXPERT: Well, that's perfectly true, and I think it is our job today to try and value them really. What am I going to say for the best Swiss enamel gold snuffbox I have ever seen in my life? £120,000 . . . And then for a Prussian gold snuffbox, a highly figurative one, highly imaginative one . . . £225,000. And then the companion piece, how can it be worth less? Then, perhaps most spectacularly of all, the Emperor's gold cigar case from pre-revolutionary Russia by Fabergé . . . £320,000. So what you have brought me today is a grand total of . . . £890,000.

JOE *looks straight into the camera, grins broadly and does a thumbs up.*

INT. RECEPTION ROOM. ELLIOT'S HOUSE. NIGHT
ELLIOT *and* JOE *are sitting at opposite ends of the table in*
ELLIOT*'s reception room, eating pâté. There are a whole selection*
of pâtés spread out across the table. They are munching their
way through them.

ELLIOT: They didn't tell you any more than that?
JOE: No.

> ELLIOT *stares at the animal snuffboxes, almost an anxious*
> *look. Then he smiles.*

ELLIOT: I am sure they've got a story to tell . . . (*Turning*
back to JOE.) And no other adventures there?
JOE: No.
ELLIOT: And what about here? Are they coming this week?
JOE: Not sure . . .
ELLIOT: How often do they use the house?

> JOE, *pretending not to hear, eats his pâté.*

ELLIOT: Not going to tell me how often they visit? That's
your business, is it?
JOE: Yes.
ELLIOT (*smiles*): Quite right . . . that's right, Joe. You know,
if you ever want to have a friend stay over in the
house yourself – you can. You can invite who you
want, whenever you want.
JOE: Thanks . . .
ELLIOT: It might make a change.
JOE: I'll think about it . . .

> JOE *stands up, ready to leave.*

ELLIOT: And if you want to eat at the lobster restaurant,
you can use the red card there you know. It'll go
straight on my account. Feel free. Invite a friend.
JOE (*moving*): Thanks.
ELLIOT: Where are you going?
JOE: Thought I'd go now . . .

ELLIOT: Just a moment . . . I want to give you a present
    for helping me out –

JOE (*by door*): I don't need a present.

ELLIOT: Don't worry – you might not want this present . . .

INT. STORAGE ROOM. NIGHT

*A light goes on with a sharp flick in a stark storage room. There
is just one old Formica table in the middle of the room. On the
table there is a great quantity of fluffy toys, huge jokey stereo
headphones, some in the shape of bumblebees and ladybirds,
garden gnomes, slippers in the shapes of turtles' and frogs' feet,
lots of comedy hats and wigs and a couple of small televisions
rather incongruously perched in the corner.*

    JOE, *who has come into the room very cautiously, stares at
the table in total surprise.* ELLIOT *picks up one of the comedy
hats and turns it over his hand.*

ELLIOT: When you're wealthy and people want to say
    thank you – if you've helped them out – and they
    want to give you a gift . . . a lot of people for some
    reason seem to think a comedy present is the best
    idea – because of course they assume I've got simply
    everything I could possibly want . . . (*He moves the
    objects on the table.*) So I get an awful lot of these
    things . . . Anything you want?

    JOE *stares at the pile, his eyes flick across the objects. He
    smiles.*

JOE: Maybe . . . yes!

INT. THE LARGE HOUSE. LATE AFTERNOON

We see JOE *wearing the enormous bumblebee headphones. They
have antennae sticking out and make him look extraordinary.*

We hear the music he is listening to, a rippling sensual loud rock track.

Suddenly he sees the front door being opened by one of the cleaners who is on the point of leaving. CHARLOTTE *is standing on the step in her red dress. She looks dazzling.* JOE *beams and indicates to the* MAID *to let her in.*

CHARLOTTE: I am a little early . . .
> *She looks embarrassed as the* MAID *leaves, then she smiles at* JOE *in his huge headphones.*

CHARLOTTE: Those are great! (*She raises her voice because the music is still pounding on the soundtrack.*) I AM SORRY I'M EARLY.
> JOE *is staring at her, with the music blaring in his ears. She looks intoxicating. He turns the music down a bit but leaves it playing. He doesn't take the headphones off, but just looks at* CHARLOTTE *and smiles a delighted smile. There is a knock on the front door and* CHARLOTTE *opens it to let* RICHARD *in. They both stand smiling at* JOE *in his enormous headphones. All we can hear is the music. And then they begin to climb the stairs.* JOE *watches them go, in a flowing dance-like movement of the camera, as the music pounds out in his ears.*

INT. THE BEDROOM WITH TROPICAL BIRDS. LATE AFTERNOON
We cut inside the bedroom. CHARLOTTE *is laughing, pointing to the bedside table. There is a whole deli selection of cold meats, cheese, biscuits and a jar of pickled onions.*

CHARLOTTE: Look what Joe's done –
RICHARD: He's provided a feast!
> CHARLOTTE *takes a pickled onion out of the jar.*

CHARLOTTE: If you love me . . . you'll kiss me after I've
eaten this . . .
She eats the onion slowly, crunching it, looking straight at
RICHARD *as she does so.* RICHARD *immediately takes her*
in his arms and gives her a long, lingering kiss.
RICHARD: You see, I didn't even hesitate . . .
We stay on CHARLOTTE'S *eyes, studying him.*

INT. HALL/BEDROOM. EVENING
We cut back to JOE *in his enormous headphones. The music has*
changed, he has selected something intimate and deeply felt.
  He moves along the hall trailing his arm along the walls, as
we cut back to CHARLOTTE *and* RICHARD *in a naked embrace,*
making love.

INT. HALL. DUSK
The light is falling. JOE *is sitting as his desk.* CHARLOTTE *comes*
down the stairs. JOE *is waiting for her, without the headphones.*
He stands up.

CHARLOTTE: Goodnight, Joe.
JOE: Goodnight . . .
  But instead of leaving, CHARLOTTE *moves towards him.*
CHARLOTTE: I won't be seeing you for a while, Joe . . .
maybe for a long while . . .
  JOE *immediately looks very worried.*
JOE: What do you mean?
CHARLOTTE: I am going away next week for a family
holiday . . . with my husband and the kids. And then
. . . Anyway, I don't know when I'll be back here . . .
  JOE *can't conceal how devastated he is by the news.*
JOE: You will be back, though?

CHARLOTTE: That's a difficult question, Joe. After the holidays . . . I have no idea what will happen in the autumn . . . (*She ruffles his hair fondly.*) I wish you could tell me!

JOE *stares at her.*

JOE: You gotta come back! This can't be the last time!

CHARLOTTE: Don't look like that, Joe.

She takes him in her arms, hugs him close, his head on her breast. JOE *holds on to her really tightly, wanting her to stay.*

CHARLOTTE: Take care of yourself . . . don't let the spooky man upset you . . .

JOE *is still holding on to her, his face pressed against her.*

CHARLOTTE: Really really take care of yourself, Joe . . .

We stay on JOE*'s face as she holds him tightly to her body.*

INT. ORIENTAL FISH RESTAURANT. NIGHT

Wide shot of JOE *sitting alone at a table in the middle of the oriental fish restaurant.*

He is tucking into two lobsters. The restaurant is not very busy and the few diners that are there keep glancing at this large boy cracking open the lobsters, sending bits of shell sprinkling all over the table.

JOE *looks up as he bites into a bit of claw. He stares straight out.*

We cut to an image of CHARLOTTE *looking at him.*

A waiter passes.

JOE: I will sign for the food now . . .

EXT. CENTRAL LONDON STREETS. NIGHT

We see JOE *patrolling the night streets, jangling his large bunch of keys. He is moving through the West End at night. The shots have a vivid vérité feel, as we see people queuing for clubs, couples walking hand in hand, drunken faces, a sense of swirling, edgy night life.*

JOE *keeps looking for single people out on their own, a girl in a doorway on her mobile phone, another young woman standing outside a restaurant, a beautiful girl wandering down a side street. She glances behind her at* JOE *with cold eyes.*

JOE *sees two chubby boys standing gossiping on a street corner; he watches from the other side of the road jangling his keys, wandering if he should interrupt them.*

The sound blurs, a series of faces passing JOE, *moving through the night city locked in their own worlds.*

INT. HALL OF THE LARGE HOUSE. NIGHT
We see JOE *coming back into the hall of the large house. There is a glow of a lighted cigarette in the dark. It is the* SECURITY GUARD.

JOE: Night, Harry . . .
    The SECURITY GUARD *hunches his shoulders, takes a drag and grunts a goodnight.*

INT. THE DELICATESSEN. LATE AFTERNOON
We see JOE *entering the deli in the evening sun, just as it is about to close. He stands at the counter, with his large bunch of keys.*

TINA: What are you choosing today then? (*She smiles.*)
    Four kilos of Parma ham that will take me a week to slice?!
    JOE *looks at* TINA *and jangles his keys.*
JOE: Want to spend a night at the big house?
TINA (*startled*): No, thank you! I wouldn't!

JOE: Why not?

TINA: Jesus, Joe, just because you've got his red card for the cheese doesn't mean you can come in and rattle a bunch of keys in my face and say how about it? In the big house?!

JOE: You're wrong – it's not for that. I thought you might like to see the house . . . Aren't you interested in history?

TINA (*laughs*): I'm very interested in history, as it happens – (*Seeing* JOE*'s disbelieving face.*) Yeah! Just not sure what's that got to do with it, though . . . (JOE *is already staring out into the street.*) Joe, you're not going to try and pick up anybody off the street – ? Be careful! (JOE *is moving.*) Why don't you go home, Joe, see your family?

JOE: Because I've got a whole house I can use, that's why!

EXT. WEST END STREET. NIGHT

JOE *patrolling the streets, looking for companionship, stopping and staring each time he sees somebody likely, out on their own. An even edgier feel than the night before.*

JOE (*voice-over*): Tonight I had a real surprise, I was out looking for somebody that might want to see the house . . . when suddenly – there he was . . .
We see ELLIOT *walking on his own, in the opposite direction down the West End street.*

JOE (*voice-over*): Maybe he was also looking . . . the funny thing is, we nodded to each other, like it was a really usual thing . . . and then we went on our way, like we shouldn't disturb each other.

I couldn't help looking back, though.
We see JOE *turn and watch* ELLIOT *moving anonymously and on his own through the crowds in the West End.*

INT. JOE'S ROOM AT THE LARGE HOUSE. NIGHT
We cut to JOE *sitting on his bed in his room in the big house,
opposite the wombat picture. He is on his mobile phone; it is
dialling.*

INT. STAIRCASE. SMALL HOUSE/JOE'S ROOM. NIGHT
We see CHARLOTTE *in a nightdress sitting on the top of a small
staircase, as if in a holiday cottage. We can hear children's
voices shouting at each other excitedly.*

JOE (*voice-over*): Hi, Charlotte . . .
CHARLOTTE: Joe . . . ?!
JOE (*voice-over*): Yeah, just thought I'd call –
CHARLOTTE: I can't talk now . . . it's really late and the
        kids are still awake . . .
        We can hear the kids' voices calling excitedly, really loud.
JOE (*voice-over*): Yeah, I can hear them.
CHARLOTTE: What is it you wanted?
JOE (*voice-over*): Nothing. Nothing really. (*Rather suavely.*)
        Just saying hello . . .
CHARLOTTE: I can't talk now! Take care, Joe . . .
        He rings off. We stay on his eyes. He sees an image of
        RICHARD *and* CHARLOTTE *running along the top passage
        of the house, laughing together. Then an image of*
        CHARLOTTE *in a tight dress walking towards him, putting
        her arms round him like she did in the kitchen and
        holding him close, his head on her breast.*

INT. ELLIOT'S BEDROOM AND PASSAGE. EVENING
We cut to ELLIOT *tying his tie in a mirror in his cluttered
bedroom. The room is full of pictures he has done propped up
against the wall. And Post-it notes plastered on the chest of
drawers and even on the bedstead. There are pictures of*

landscapes, an intense picture of the castle with the moat and
also of cattle, fine studies of cows' faces staring at us.

ELLIOT: You think this suit is good, Laarni? . . . The right
    choice?
The Filipino maid is standing in the doorway.
LAARNI: Oh yes, sir.
ELLIOT: You know this picture they're doing . . . I can't
    believe everybody is going to turn up, apparently it is
    a sort of photographic Holy Grail – getting the eight
    richest people in Britain together at the same time,
    standing like in a school photo . . . !

    I hate the idea of going, Laarni . . . but I've got to
    get out more! After all, I used to! (*He smiles.*) Women
    too, Laarni! Had some great times . . . And what can
    go wrong? I'll just smile at everybody . . .

EXT. WEST END STREET. DUSK
We cut to JOE *moving down another street in the West End,*
a less busy street. There are two young people in blankets curled
up in a couple of doorways. One a very pale boy, with tiny eyes
blinking rapidly, the other a blond boy with an intelligent face.
    JOE *goes up to the blond boy* (JASON), *jangling his keys.*

JOE: Want somewhere to stay tonight? I look after a big
    house . . . you want to see it?
JASON: What do you want for it?
JOE: Nothing. Don't want anything. No money . . . no
    payment of any kind.
JASON (*stretches*): I'll think about the house . . . I wouldn't
    mind a meal though.
JOE (*rattling his keys*): A meal? . . . Sure, I can do that.
    That's no problem either.
    JASON *stands up, unwrapping himself from the blanket.*

JASON: Not what you expected?!

> JOE *is indeed surprised to see the boy is wearing a pin-striped suit, albeit slightly worn.*

JASON: Like the suit? Not bad, is it?! (*He smiles.*) Actually it's fucking cold down there – don't know how people do it all the time. They must be crazy! Why don't they bring a fucking mattress?! (*As he passes the other boy.*) Ever thought of that ?! (*To* JOE.) OK, take me for the meal . . .

> *As they move off they pass a large yellow metal police 'scene of crime' notice, standing in the middle of the pavement.*

Yeah, a fat guy was stabbed here last week . . . great big fat guy, he was on the pavement right here . . . (*Breezily.*) I once was in a street, there were five of these police notices in the very same street! This is true – there had been five stabbings on the same street. I took a picture . . . I'll show it to you later . . . (*He looks around.*) Where are you taking me? If I don't like the food I won't stay, I warn you . . .

JOE: You'll like the food.

EXT. STREET. NIGHT

ELLIOT*'s Mercedes draws up outside a modern building.* ELLIOT *is sitting on the back seat. He swallows hard with nerves.*

ELLIOT (*to his driver*): Just wait here, Simon . . . I might be out at any time . . . (*He opens the door but doesn't immediately get out.*) Got to make myself . . . (*He climbs out of the car.*) Absolutely dreading it . . . total dread.

> *We cut to* ELLIOT *heading up the steps towards the large glass doors of the building. He looks incredibly anxious.*

He mutters to himself.
Just let me not be the first, please. (*Nervous smile.*)
If there is a God – don't let me be first!

INT. MODERN PASSAGE AND CONFERENCE ROOM. NIGHT
We cut to ELLIOT *being led by a young woman down a modern passage and into a large room where there is a black backdrop and photographic lights. There is a series of low plinths for the rich men to stand on in front of the backdrop. There are a cluster of PR people and young assistants milling around. There is a table of drinks and in the middle of the room a loose huddle of the seven richest men in Britain – a rather nondescript group of middle-aged men.* ELLIOT *looks by far the most stylish man there.*

ELLIOT (*to the young woman*): Blimey . . . Is that what we
  look like . . . grey men in crumpled suits?!
  We see the event through ELLIOT's *eyes in a series of dissolves, as people ply him with drinks, and move him backwards and forwards introducing him to the other participants. He notices the clump of middle-aged men eyeing each other with cold eyes and making desultory small talk.*
      A JOURNALIST *comes up to* ELLIOT *with a big smile.*
  ELLIOT *is beginning to hyperventilate with the tension of meeting all these new people.*
JOURNALIST: So glad you could make it, Mr Graham. It's
  going to be a historic picture!
ELLIOT: Everybody has turned up! . . . I don't know why
  we have!
JOURNALIST: Yes – it's great. People have been trying to do
  this picture for years and now we have managed it.
  We'll be doing the interviews afterwards.
ELLIOT (*looking very startled and anxious*): Interview?!
  I didn't know there was going be an interview . . . !

(*He raises his voice and addresses the others, the nerves are making him blurt things out.*) When you see us all together . . . you realise what an odd-looking bunch we really are!! (*He chuckles as everybody looks at him.*) How are we going to decide who's on which step? Who goes at the front? Is it done by who's worth most?! . . . At around four billion I am a mere minnow, I think . . . a mere stickleback! (*He smiles.*) I'll be at the back . . .

JOURNALIST (*startled*): Shall I get you another drink, Mr Graham?

ELLIOT: No, just stay here . . . I am feeling a trifle nervous . . . I ought to stop talking, oughtn't I?! (*But he can't stop himself calling out to the others again.*) I am not sure I know any of you, do I?

They look at him.

I always wonder about the kids – do any of you do that? . . . (*He smiles.*) You know, the next generation . . . with all these billionaires in the country – what's happening to the children?! I am a kid of the super-rich and I am definitely not normal. As you may have noticed! Fortunately I don't have kids . . . Who's got a normal kid here?! (*He calls out merrily.*) Anybody got a normal kid?!

The room is beginning to fall silent. Everybody is looking at ELLIOT. *He goes on.*

Tell you what would make this picture even better . . . I've got a great idea, you'll like this! (*Self-deprecating smile.*) You probably think I am going to say do it naked . . . but it's even better than doing it naked – though I know that's very popular at the moment and maybe we should . . . (*He grins.*) But this is a great idea – just listen to this! Because I am not a UK citizen, I hardly pay any tax, rather extraordinary state of affairs – unique to this place – that's why we are all

in this city . . . instead of the US or some other place –
that's why we've come to London, might as well be
honest! So . . . when they take the picture – (*he grins
at his own idea*) we should all be crying out 'Tax us . . .
for crying out loud, tax us!'
Everybody is staring at him in astonishment.
That would cause a stir – (*he giggles*) us all holding up
placards. 'Tax us! Tax us! Tax us!' I am a bit of an
artist as it happens . . . I could do them for us!
There is a total silence. ELLIOT *grins.*
It's a bit like I've got a sudden attack of Tourette's,
isn't it?! (*He looks at them.*) Just can't stop talking and
saying completely the wrong thing! So I think I better
. . . just make . . . a little call . . . just say . . . it was
good to meet you!

INT./EXT. MODERN BUILDING. NIGHT
We see ELLIOT *hurtling down the passage. He goes through a
door marked 'Exit', finds himself out of the back of the building,
by a building site.*

*We see him in wide shot dwarfed by cranes and working
lights and concrete walls.*

*He moves for a moment backwards and forwards, utterly lost,
trying to work out where he is.*

ELLIOT: Blimey! What on earth was I doing?!
*We see him staring around, utterly bewildered at his own
behaviour.*

INT. ELLIOT'S CAR. NIGHT
*We cut to the interior of the Mercedes. The chauffeur sees in the
driving mirror the sight of* ELLIOT *running as if for his life
towards the car. He leaps in.*

ELLIOT: Simon! Drive! Drive, for God's sake! Quick . . . !
I just made such a spectacle of myself . . . ! I was just
so completely ludicrous!
We stay on ELLIOT's *face in the back of the car.*

EXT./INT. THE LARGE HOUSE. NIGHT
JOE *unlocking the door into the night hallway.* JASON *looks up
at the exterior of the house; he seems in an increasingly wired
state.* JOE *hesitates for a second before pushing the door open.*

JASON: Never noticed this house before . . . I know
London well – but I've never seen this place before.
JOE *and* JASON *go into the hall, which is in semi-darkness.*
JOE *is hoping to show the place off.* JASON *whistles.*
JASON: This is a creepy place . . . this is fucking creepy!
You really sleep here?
JOE: Yes. Some days. I like it. I'll show you round, it's very
big –
JASON *is staring up at the staircase.*
JASON: Jesus, this is a scary place! (*Suddenly his voice begins
to rise.*) There are bad vibes here . . . There're some
very bad vibes . . . !
JOE: It's fine. It really is –
JASON *looks at him with glassy eyes.*
JASON: Why did you bring me here, Joe? Thought you'd
scare me . . . ?
JOE: No. If you don't like it, maybe you should go –
JASON: You want me to leave now, do you?! That's
interesting, because I seem to remember you begging
me to come here . . .
He produces a knife, flicking it out towards JOE.
JASON: Why do you want me to go now, Joe?
JOE (*trying not to appear scared*): Because you don't like it
here, so I thought it better you went –

JASON: That's for me to decide! When you've been to as many places as I have – I've got my own way of deciding where I stay, and you might not want to find out what that is . . . (*He begins to trail his arm along the banister, his voice becoming a rambling mutter.*) When I went to France, they liked everything I did, offered me a four-year contract, paid holidays as well. Same hotel as Tom Cruise stays in . . .

As soon as JASON has turned away from him, JOE runs off along the passage calling out.

JOE: Harry . . . Harry! Where are you?! (*He can hear JASON shouting out for him.*) HARRY . . . !

JOE bangs violently on the door of HARRY, the security guard, then pushes it open. HARRY is slumped asleep in his chair surrounded by empty cans of beer. JOE yells at him.

JOE: HARRY!

JOE shakes him desperately; HARRY fails to respond. JASON's voice is screaming after JOE, piercing shouts echoing round the building.

JASON (*calling*): Don't run away from me, Joe . . . come here . . . !

JOE comes out into the darkened passage. JASON is right the other end of the passage with his knife. He is yelling in a highly disturbing fashion.

JASON: You come here right now, right *here*! – and tell me why you want me to leave? . . . And I'll show what I want to do about that! . . .

JOE stares at the advancing JASON, totally uncertain what to do. Suddenly the front door opens. There, silhouetted against the street light, is ELLIOT. Framed in the doorway, he looks terrifying.

ELLIOT: I heard shouting in my house . . .

JASON turns, very alarmed, seeing this frightening-looking figure.

ELLIOT*'s voice rumbles towards him in a tone that cannot be contradicted.*

ELLIOT: Get out of my house! GET OUT OF MY HOUSE RIGHT NOW . . .

JASON *dashes out into the night like a frightened dog.*

JOE *looks across at* ELLIOT. *very relieved.*

JOE: Thank you, Mr Graham . . .

ELLIOT (*smiles*): It seemed to work, didn't it?!

JOE: Yes! If you hadn't come . . . not sure what would have happened . . . Harry is drunk.

Sharp cut. The door of HARRY*'s office opens.* ELLIOT *sees the slumped shape of the security guard.*

ELLIOT: He certainly is . . . we must get you better protection, Joe. But maybe, for now, we can borrow his beer.

There is one six-pack HARRY *has not managed to drink.*

INT. BALLROOM. NIGHT

ELLIOT *and* JOE *are sitting on the floor of the empty ballroom, a little apart, drinking beer.* ELLIOT *takes a long swig.*

ELLIOT: I've had a terrible night tonight, too, Joe . . .

JOE (*drinking*): Sorry to hear that.

ELLIOT: I made an idiot of myself. (*Self-deprecating smile.*) I was like somebody who'd been let out of an institution after twenty years in solitary!

JOE (*slightly baffled by this*): Right . . .

ELLIOT (*drinking, glancing around*): I don't know why I don't like this house. But I don't – maybe there are too many ghosts here, people I remember . . .

JOE: There are no ghosts here, Mr Graham.

ELLIOT (*smiles*): Right, Joe . . . None of any kind?

JOE: No. There aren't. Nothing to be scared of . . .

ELLIOT: I'll try to remember that, Joe . . . You're right, I
    must spend more time here, mustn't I? Come on a
    visit – see everybody again.

INT. HALLWAY. DAY
The staff are excited, all lined up in the hall. They are talking to
each other and glancing at the door. There are six cleaners, MRS
HOPKINS *and* JOE, *forming a reception party.*
    There is a modest knock on the door.

MRS HOPKINS: Open the door, Joe.
JOE: He's got a key. He'll let himself in.
MRS HOPKINS: Open the door!
    JOE *opens the door,* ELLIOT *is standing there with a tall*
    young man a couple of paces behind him. The tall man is
    holding two rusty cans of 35mm film.

ELLIOT: Hello, Joe . . . Hello, everybody!

The cleaners all greet him.

MRS HOPKINS: It's very good to see you, Mr Graham.

ELLIOT: Yes. It's been far too long. (*He smiles at them all.*)
The floor looks marvellous . . . everything is so clean,
cleaner then I've ever seen it. It's very pleasing . . . the
flowers too . . . excellent!

MRS HOPKINS and the cleaners smile back.

ELLIOT: So who's going to join me for a little film show in
the cinema? A chance to have a break?

The very tall man looms behind ELLIOT *with the film
cans.*

ELLIOT: As you see, Philip has got some films with him . . .
Who's going to join us?

*The cleaners faces fall, they shift around as if they have to
get back to work immediately.*

MRS HOPKINS: I'm sorry, I'm a little busy today for the
films, Mr Graham . . . and I think the rest of the staff
may have too much to do too . . .

ELLIOT (*looking at the reluctant faces*): Really? (*He smiles.*)
Too busy for the film show? Do we really have no
takers at all . . . ? How about you, Joe?

JOE, who has been fiddling with his keys, looks up.

JOE: Sure . . . I can come.

INT. CINEMA. DAY

We cut to ELLIOT *and* JOE *sitting next to each other in the
plush red seats in the miniature cinema. The house lights begin
to go down.*

ELLIOT: We should have ice cream or some popcorn,
shouldn't we?

JOE (*producing amaretti sweets*): I've got a few of these.

ELLIOT: Thanks. Most kind. My father built this to show
    Hollywood films! To impress his friends . . . What do
    you think we're going to see, Joe?

JOE: Big epic sort of thing? The pyramids? –

ELLIOT: The pyramids? No, Joe.

JOE: Battle scenes then? Pirates in space, fighting in the
    galaxy – that'd be good!

ELLIOT: No, not quite. (*He smiles.*) Definitely not pirates
    in space. Just a lot of old street scenes, in fact . . .
    JOE*'s face falls.*

ELLIOT: Yes! (*He chuckles.*) That's why nobody wanted to
    come!
    The curtains part on the screen.
    You know I watch a lot of movies, a lot of TV,
    especially the old ones – I have the time! And I always
    find myself looking at the backgrounds when the film
    goes outside . . . you know, the old cars, the clothes,
    people's faces, the old buildings . . . So this is a bit of
    a personal whim of mine . . . Because I sometimes
    give money to film archives, I've been able to get hold
    of a lot of this stuff, film they shot to be in the
    background of the story . . . which they call phantom
    rides, Joe.

JOE (*very dubious*): Right . . . That's all it is, then?
    *The film begins. Vivid travelling shots, either filmed from
    the front or the back of a moving vehicle, driving through
    city streets of the thirties and forties.*

    *The camera is always moving, we are floating along old
    streets with vehicles looming right up in our face, people
    rushing very close to the camera. We travel along tramlines,
    climb up towards the light from subterranean tram stations,
    we swing round the corner of a thirties street to be plunged
    right into a traffic jam, we travel along the side of the
    Thames with other trams rumbling really close to us,*

bearing down on us out of the smog. We swerve sideways
suddenly past a pedestrian crossing with a policeman's face
turned towards us, calling.

    We are immediately right there in the past. The shots
are accompanied by an evocative but powerful soundtrack
of voices and sounds of the period. There is also music,
both from the past and modern, cues which slide into each
other giving the images a contemporary force.

ELLIOT: Because the camera is always moving, Joe, I find
    the brain moves with it – it's how we see things now,
    from a car or a bus . . . (*he smiles*) not that I've been
    on a bus recently, Joe! So you really find yourself
    time-travelling . . . I've had some sound added, of
    course, which I think works quite well . . .
    We move in close on ELLIOT.
    And you do feel, don't you, you're riding into the
    past? Don't you, Joe?
    JOE *staring at the shots, intrigued, being half drawn in.*

JOE: Yeah . . . Are they very long, these ghost rides?

ELLIOT: Phantom rides . . . (*He smiles.*) As long as we
    want, Joe. Do you feel you're really there?

JOE: A bit . . . (*Staring up at the screen.*) Once or twice . . .

ELLIOT: I think it's because you're squashed up close to
    things . . . they come nearer than you expect.
    We see a London bus from the 1940s looming right up to
    us, bearing down until it gets uncomfortably close.

ELLIOT: This is the landscape of my father's youth . . . the
    streets where he was young . . . because somehow I've
    got to face the past, Joe, find out if there is anything
    I need really worry about . . .
    JOE *is staring up at the screen.*

JOE: You're looking for something then? Up there?

ELLIOT: In a way. I'm looking for a bit of courage, I
    suppose . . . and energy! Ever since my father died six
    years ago I've been trying to do that . . .

We see the camera travelling down rural roads, swinging past people working in the fields.

I like this bit . . . I was just a farmer, Joe, with a rather ramshackle farm while my father was alive, while he was busy running his fortune . . . (*He grins.*) I was Farmer Elliot . . . I love cattle . . . (*He smiles.*) I love animals in general, but cattle in particular . . .

JOE *glances sideways; he sees* ELLIOT *has become affected by the films, his tone quite emotional.*

ELLIOT: So I feel I've got to get to grips with how I've ended up who I am . . . (*He is staring up at the screen.*) Until I do – it's like everything is blocked . . . I'm stuck, Joe – can't go forward! After all, with the money I've got – what I could do! I could help with disease in Africa like others are doing . . . I could help contribute to conservation . . . (*Slight smile.*) I could help save things and build things . . .

JOE: You could.

ELLIOT: I could!

They plunge along the streets of the past as they stare at the screen.

We move in close on ELLIOT, *an emotional, troubled look in his eyes.*

ELLIOT: I need to discover more, Joe . . . about my father . . . about his money. (*He is staring at the screen.*) I'm thinking all the time, I can't spend the money until I know about it . . . until I understand completely how it was all made. And that is surprisingly difficult to find out.

The images on the screen burst into colour.

JOE: That's good!

ELLIOT: Yes, isn't it?! (*Glancing at the boy.*) You don't have to spend time with me, you know, Joe . . .

JOE: No, it's OK.

*The images on the screen ride on, pulling them into the
past.* JOE *is watching intently.*
This is quite good now . . .
The screen dissolves to white.

EXT. THE PARK. DAY
We see emerging out of the white dissolve ELLIOT *and* JOE
coming towards us along a broad path in a London park. JOE
is walking slightly apart from ELLIOT, *jangling his keys. They
walk for a moment in silence. We can hear faint music drifting
towards them from across the park.*

JOE (*voice-over*): I went out for a walk with him today –
(*He glances sideways at* ELLIOT.) I keep thinking about
him killing people with his bare hands, and whether
he really did it or not, and if he'll do it again – (*He
turns to* ELLIOT *in the park.*) Were you in the army,
Mr Graham?

ELLIOT: I was . . . When I was very young I buried myself
in the army for seven years – (*he smiles*) to stop myself
having to worry about who I was . . .
Slight pause.

JOE: Did you wear gloves in the army?

ELLIOT: Gloves? No. Not as a rule.

JOE: Right . . .
The music is louder. Dance music.

ELLIOT: Hear that? I was hoping that was happening
today. I saw it before. You know, when you don't go
out much like me, Joe, when you do everything seems
rather bright and vivid, and you see strange things . . .
like this –
*They turn a corner. There is some alfresco dancing
happening in the park, people paying for dance classes*

*and then taking part in a dance. The dance floor is in
a clearing in the park; the music is coming out of speakers.*

At the moment ELLIOT *and* JOE *come across them,
about twelve couples are dancing together.*

For a moment they stand and watch the dancers.

ELLIOT (*looking at the couples*): You can't really tell if they
know each other or if they're complete strangers can
you . . . ?

Suddenly they see they know one of the dancers. TINA *is
dancing with a very short young man.*

JOE: Tina! Never thought she'd be doing this!

We cut to the dance finishing. TINA *thanks the very short
man who is obviously a complete stranger. She sees* JOE
and ELLIOT *and immediately approaches them.*

TINA: Joe! Mr Graham!

ELLIOT (*obviously pleased to see her*): Tina, very good to see
you out and about, away from all the cheeses!

TINA: Yeah . . . I like coming here. (*She stares at the two
men.*) Since I don't suppose I am going to get either
of you to dance – want to come and sit over here? I've
got some fruit . . .

*We cut to the three of them sitting together in the shade
under a tree, eating some cherries.*

The next dance has started. JOE *is staring at the couples
dancing.*

For a moment he imagines CHARLOTTE *and* RICHARD
dancing together, a really stylish couple in the park.

TINA*'s voice suddenly cuts through. She is looking
straight at* ELLIOT.

TINA: What do you do all day, Mr Graham? When you are
not eating stuff from the deli?

ELLIOT (*not offended by her directness*): Good question!
I receive a lot of reports on my money of course . . .
and I am trying to get somebody to make sense of my
father's archives, find out about his financial history.

I keep hiring different people but I am not sure
they're getting at the truth –

JOE (*loud teasing tone*): You should get Tina to do it! The
way she slices the salami she would get through it all
right!

ELLIOT *chuckles at this.* JOE *warms to his theme.*

JOE: And she likes history too, doesn't she?

TINA *ignores their laughter.*

TINA: What do you want doing? (*She looks straight at*
ELLIOT.) Whatever it is, I could have a try.

INT. NARROW ROOM. ELLIOT'S HOUSE. DAY
TINA *and* ELLIOT *staring down at all the boxes in the narrow
room. The walls are covered with pictures of the large house and
the castle in the country.*

ELLIOT: These are the most important boxes, all my father's
diaries and letters. There are some more boxes in the
big house – I will have them brought over.

TINA: OK. (*She peers into the boxes.*) I'll start reading this
lot then, every page. I'll do it three days a week, I'm
still going to do two at the deli – so it will take me
quite a while, Mr Graham . . .

    TINA *kneels by the boxes, begins glancing at the papers.*

ELLIOT: Right. I see. (*Smiles.*) Keeping the deli on just in
case . . . (*He indicates the papers.*) Lots of people have
gone through these already, of course. If you read
their findings and then anything you uncover that
doesn't fit, or contradicts them, you let me know.
(*A shadow crosses his face.*) I just feel they may have
missed something.

TINA (*grins*): And you think *I'll* spot it?

ELLIOT: On the face of it, it seems quite unlikely, Tina, but –

TINA: But worth a try?! (*She smiles.*) I agree!

EXT./INT. FRONT DOOR. LARGE HOUSE. DUSK
The panel slides open. CHARLOTTE *is standing there in a
winter coat. It is dusk.*

CHARLOTTE: Hello, Joe.

    JOE *is staring at her through the panel. Thrilled to see her.
He smiles a big smile.*

JOE (*voice-over*): They came back today. At first it was
really great! And then something odd happened . . .

INT. KITCHEN. DUSK
RICHARD *is moving around the kitchen, his mood rather febrile.*
CHARLOTTE *is sitting quietly, self-contained. The light is falling.*

RICHARD: How I've missed this kitchen! All these superb
pots, it looks like some of them haven't been used for
fifty years, doesn't it, Charlotte?!

CHARLOTTE *is sitting quietly, not reacting to* RICHARD.

RICHARD: And these wonderful bundles of colour
supplements of the 1960s – Elliot obviously can't bear
to throw anything out! (*He turns.*) And I've missed
you, Joe.

CHARLOTTE: Of course . . .

RICHARD: He looks terrific, doesn't he?!

In fact JOE *looks rather pale.*

RICHARD: There's something new about you, Joe . . . Is it
your hair? Something's changed? Tell me your news –

JOE: Lot's been happening! There's a new security guard
called Martin, he says even less than the last one . . .
Harry was a drunk, though, but I think Martin stays
awake. Some of the cleaners have left, and my mum's
gone to Spain – she sends me postcards. And Mr
Graham has hired Tina, the girl from the deli, to go
through his father's papers because the historians
failed to –

RICHARD (*loud, incredulous*): He hasn't?! The girl from the
deli? He hasn't done that!

JOE: Yes.

RICHARD: That's wonderful, isn't it, Charlotte, the girl
from the deli to do his research?! He really has gone
insane now! (*Turns.*) Don't you think, Joe?

JOE *hesitates.*

JOE: Mr Elliot's not mad . . . he's a bit –

RICHARD (*his tone very sharp suddenly, darkly impatient*):
Oh, come on, Joe! You're worth billions, you can do
absolutely anything you want – and what do you
choose to do? You sit around eating salami and pâté
all day and you become so obsessed with the deli you

get the girl from behind the counter to go through
your papers! That is totally, totally bonkers. You've got
to admit that, Joe?

Pause. Close-up of JOE.

JOE: Yeah . . .

RICHARD: That's right, Joe. He's finally gone!

JOE: Maybe you should pay him a visit . . . see what you
think, if he is mad or –

RICHARD (*coldly*): Jesus, no! I don't want to have to see the
scary guy unless I really have to!

Suddenly he turns to CHARLOTTE, *almost impatiently.*

RICHARD: Come on – we've got to rechristen the room.

They begin to move. CHARLOTTE *looks up slowly.*

JOE: I put a telly in there . . . in case you wanted it!

RICHARD *turns, his tone is perfunctory now, as if to a
hotel porter.*

RICHARD: Right . . . and the heating is on and everything,
I hope?

JOE *is startled by* RICHARD*'s offhand tone.*

JOE: Yes. Of course.

JOE *watches them go upstairs. And then we hear his voice-
over start.*

JOE (*voice-over*): Something was different . . . When they
went upstairs they weren't saying anything, weren't
smiling. Charlotte didn't even look at me.

JOE *watches them disappear from view. We track towards
his face bewildered, upset.*

INT. NARROW ROOM/PASSAGE. WINTER LIGHT
ELLIOT*'s father's papers are spreading out of the narrow room
and into the passage, forming a long paper trail of neat piles.*
TINA *is kneeling on the floor in the passage staring at the
papers.*

INT. JOE'S BEDROOM. LARGE HOUSE. DAY
We track in on JOE's *face, at a disorientating angle.*

His eyes flick open. He sees there is snow right up against the window of his downstairs room, a sludge of snow and dead leaves. The cat is moving around the courtyard in the snow.

JOE *is lying on his bed, fully clothed. He looks pale and drawn as if he hasn't been out for weeks.*

Suddenly he senses something and turns his head.

CHARLOTTE *is standing in the doorway of his room in her winter coat.*

JOE: It's you!

CHARLOTTE: Hello, Joe.

    JOE *is sitting up in his bed, blinking.*

JOE: Sorry – I was just having an afternoon nap. It was so quiet I thought I could. I didn't know you were coming!

CHARLOTTE: Neither did I. I was just passing. One of the girls let me in. It's only me today.

JOE: Right . . . only you?

    CHARLOTTE *seems very preoccupied.*

CHARLOTTE: I'll go up. If I may. I just fancy sitting for a bit. I need to be on my own.

    Time cut. JOE *at his desk, sitting very still. The last cleaner leaves.*

    We move in on JOE. *He can hear a strange noise from upstairs, like stifled crying.*

    JOE *goes upstairs. Then along the passage. The door of the bedroom with bird wallpaper is open. We track with him as he approaches silently.*

    CHARLOTTE *is sitting on the end of the bed, crying. She is watching the TV, some afternoon game show.* JOE *moves a little closer. He stands in the doorway, watching her cry.*

    CHARLOTTE *looks up.*

CHARLOTTE: Joe!

> JOE *watches her for a moment.*

JOE: What's the matter?

CHARLOTTE: I am sorry. I am being very stupid.

JOE: Is it about Richard?

CHARLOTTE: No, no . . . It's certainly not about Richard.
No! (*She stares at the TV. She looks truly upset.*)
Sometimes I'm just . . .

JOE: Yes?

CHARLOTTE: So full of fear, Joe . . .

JOE: About what?

CHARLOTTE: For my kids . . . how to keep them safe – lots
of things . . . (*She looks straight at* JOE.) So what am
I doing here? Must seem odd to you, Joe?

> JOE *is staring at her sitting on the end of the bed. Her*
> *tears still on her cheeks.*

JOE: No . . . You can come here whenever you want.

INT. KITCHEN. DAY
We cut to JOE *in the kitchen, writing in the ledger.*

JOE (*voice-over*): I'm going out less and less. I don't see Mr
Graham, but doesn't matter because she is coming
two or three times a week, on her own, just to sit in
the room and watch TV.

> *We see* CHARLOTTE *watching the news on TV, footage of*
> *fighting from the Middle East. We move in on her face.*

JOE (*voice-over*): I don't disturb her . . . but I make tea for
her.

> *We see him handing* CHARLOTTE *a mug of tea. She leans*
> *forward and kisses him on the forehead, mouthing 'Thank*
> *you'. And then we see an image of* CHARLOTTE *standing*
> *alone in the doorway of the room with the bird wallpaper,*

staring down the passage, thinking about the empty building,
as if she can sense something.
CHARLOTTE: Why is the house like this?

INT. MAIN RECEPTION ROOM. ELLIOT'S HOUSE. DAY
ELLIOT *is standing in the doorway of his reception room,*
hovering so he can intercept TINA *as she leaves.*
 TINA *comes down the passage.*

ELLIOT: There you are!
TINA: Goodnight, Mr Graham. (*She turns in the passage as*
she sees ELLIOT'*s enquiring face.*) Nothing yet. Nothing
that other people haven't found!

INT./EXT. FRONT DOOR/HALL. LARGE HOUSE. EVENING
JOE *is exchanging looks with the cat that is sitting outside on*
the ledge of one of the windows. JOE *presses his face close to the*
glass, so he is right up against the cat's face.
 JOE *looks even paler then when we saw him before.*
 There is a sharp knock on the front door and a male voice
calls: 'Joe.'
 JOE *slides the panel open.* RICHARD *smiles at him.*

RICHARD: There you are, Joe. Good. And this is Patricia . . .
 Just as when JOE *first saw* CHARLOTTE, *a woman*
appears next to RICHARD *and smiles at* JOE *through the*
panel.
RICHARD: I was hoping to show Patricia the house, Joe,
if that's all right?
 JOE *looks stunned to see* RICHARD *with another woman.*
He hesitates. RICHARD *repeats his request with an edge in*
his voice, like a command.
RICHARD: If that's all right, Joe!

JOE *opens the door.* RICHARD *moves with* PATRICIA *into the hall.* PATRICIA *looks around her, impressed.*

PATRICIA: Oh, it's lovely.

RICHARD: Yes, magnificent, isn't it?!

PATRICIA: It's like a nice old-fashioned hotel.

RICHARD (*laughing at this*): What sort of hotels do you stay in?

PATRICIA: Oh, you know, when I was little, by the seaside with my parents. No, it's great.

RICHARD: And I'll just show you the upstairs now . . . (*He moves with* PATRICIA *up the stairs, calling back to* JOE.) We're just going to look at the upstairs first, Joe – we'll have a good look. (*Sharply.*) We don't need anything . . .

We stay on JOE*'s face, totally bewildered.*

PATRICIA (*as they move up the stairs*): He's a funny sort of security guard, isn't he, but I suppose they don't really get many visitors.

JOE *moves backwards and forwards getting increasingly flustered. Then suddenly he turns. He rushes up the stairs and along the passage, heading straight to the bedroom with the tropical birds. The door is shut, he knocks abruptly.*

JOE: Mr Reece! Can you open the door, Mr Reece?! (*He bangs loudly.*) I've just got to tell you something . . . (*Very loudly.*) MR REECE!

The door opens. RICHARD *stares at* JOE, *very angry at being interrupted. Inside the room* PATRICIA *is already half undressed sitting on the bed; she covers herself.*

RICHARD: Yes, Joe?

JOE: You've got to leave, I've got a call . . . Mr Graham is coming here right now . . . !

RICHARD: So? (*Very sharp.*) So what about it, Joe . . . ?

JOE: So – you've got to leave! He's coming up here, I know. You gotta leave!

JOE *moves into the room and starts trying to tidy up the bed, trying to make* PATRICIA *move.* RICHARD *catches hold of him by the arm.*

JOE: I've got to tidy up!

RICHARD *pulls* JOE *back into the passage.*

RICHARD: Patricia – I won't be a moment . . .

We cut to RICHARD *staring down at* JOE *at the top of the stairs.* JOE *is standing a couple of steps below him.* RICHARD*'s tone is very sharp and authoritative.*

RICHARD: I want you to listen to me very carefully . . . are you doing that?

JOE *nods sullenly.*

RICHARD: You know I once said to you, you are a very clever guy . . . Do you remember me saying that?

JOE *nods, not looking at him.*

RICHARD: Well, one of the things that marks one out as being clever is being able to hold two different ideas in one's head at exactly the same time – and maybe these ideas seem to contradict each other. (*He is staring intently at* JOE.) I'm a very busy man as you know, under a lot of pressure. I am not like Mr Graham, who does nothing at all, has to take no decisions – has no responsibilities of any kind! I have to work immensely hard and sometimes I have to do certain things so I can go on functioning. So – it is possible for me to be very close to Charlotte, really close, and for me to see other people. I can be happily married, which I am, but also love Charlotte too. You follow me? Equally, it's possible for me to be very dedicated to my work, but also to need to take risks. Because if I didn't do that I would cease to be able to do anything at all. You understand that, Joe?

Pause. JOE *looks at him. Very quiet.*

JOE: I understand . . .

RICHARD: Now today we will leave – but in the future you
will be fine about it? (*Slight pause.*) Won't you?
JOE *just stares. Their eyes meet.* RICHARD*'s tone changes,
impatient.*
RICHARD: You know, Joe, I think you may have been in
this house too long . . .
JOE: I don't.

INT. A ROOM IN ELLIOT'S HOUSE. DAY
TINA *is sitting at a desk in* ELLIOT*'s house surrounded by the
little animals and the golden cigar case. She is staring at the
little animals, and then consulting various reference books. The
camera moves towards her as she works with deep concentration.*

INT. THE HALL OF THE LARGE HOUSE. EVENING
CHARLOTTE *is sitting on a high-back chair in the hall opposite*
JOE*'s desk, about twenty feet from it. She is sitting very straight.*
  JOE *is writing his ledger, but also glancing up at* CHARLOTTE
between phrases.

JOE (*voice-over*): Friday. As I write this, she is sitting
opposite me . . . I haven't told her anything, of course.
CHARLOTTE: Joe?
JOE: Yes.
CHARLOTTE: What are you writing?
JOE: Just keeping a record of what happens in the house.
CHARLOTTE: And what happens in the house apart from
me and Richard?
JOE: Mostly it's cleaning.
CHARLOTTE: And the bit that isn't cleaning?
  JOE *looks up in surprise. He cannot stop himself looking
furtive.*

CHARLOTTE: I know he has other people, Joe.

JOE (*very quiet*): You know?

CHARLOTTE: Yes. I wouldn't say he shags anything that moves . . . not quite. But he has a lot of women. He probably has other empty houses belonging to billionaires scattered about the place . . . other boys opening the door to him.

JOE looks very upset about this thought.

CHARLOTTE: And you know what, Joe?

JOE (*very quiet*): What?

CHARLOTTE: It doesn't matter. It really doesn't matter to me.

JOE stares at her. CHARLOTTE *gets up, moves towards him.*

CHARLOTTE: Are you going to write that? (*She indicates the ledger.*) 'It didn't matter to Charlotte at all.' (*She leans over and whispers in his ear.*) Don't think badly of me, Joe . . .

There is the sound of RICHARD*'s familiar knock on the front door. Immediately* CHARLOTTE *looks pleased, a look of expectancy in her eyes.*

CHARLOTTE: There he is!

JOE is still staring at her.

CHARLOTTE: Aren't you going to open the door, Joe?

INT. RECEPTION ROOM. ELLIOT'S HOUSE. NIGHT

A winter evening. It is dark outside. TINA *is working at the table in* ELLIOT*'s reception room, surrounded by mounds of papers and letters. As she works,* ELLIOT *is pacing up and down watching her.*

TINA: It's great being able to work in here, Mr Graham, but your pacing . . . it's a bit –

ELLIOT: Right, Tina. I'll stop. (*He stops by the window.*) Just
a little worried about what you might find. (*Self-
deprecating smile.*) But then I want you to find
something . . . I think.
*He glances out of a window. A lot of lights are on in the
big house. He sees the front door open and* RICHARD
leave, standing on the doorstep with JOE.

RICHARD *holds out his hand, offering a handshake.*
JOE *hesitates, then takes* RICHARD*'s hand very reluctantly.*
RICHARD *ruffles* JOE*'s hair and flashes a smile before
getting into his car and being driven away.*

ELLIOT *turns back to* TINA.

ELLIOT: Must seem odd, I know, me saying I can't do
anything until this is solved –

TINA: If there is anything to solve!

ELLIOT: I hope it's not me just making an excuse –
ELLIOT *stops. He is glancing back to the big house. He
sees* JOE *standing by a downstairs window looking
preoccupied and alone.* ELLIOT *glances upwards to the
first floor. He is about to turn away when something
catches his attention. In one of the upper windows, a
bathroom, the curtain is only half drawn, and he can see*
CHARLOTTE *wrapped in a towel, bent double as if in
pain.*

ELLIOT *watches, suddenly very concerned.*

CHARLOTTE *disappears into the shadow of the bathroom,
and then he sees her again clearly. She is holding the side
of the bath, her face seemingly contorted in real pain.*

ELLIOT: I've got to – I'll be right back, Tina!
ELLIOT *rushes out.*

INT. HALL. NIGHT
ELLIOT *moves into the hall in agitated state, calling out.*

ELLIOT: Joe! Where are you? Joe!

For a moment the downstairs seems empty.

Joe!

JOE *appears in the shadows, looking very pale.*

ELLIOT: Joe! I think the girl's in pain upstairs . . . You must help me find her! (*He starts to move up the stairs.*) You know the room they were using?

JOE *hasn't moved.*

ELLIOT: Come on . . . I think she's ill!

JOE: She was all right when she arrived.

ELLIOT: She's ill, I tell you!

We cut to them coming towards us down the first-floor passage. JOE *is now leading the way, but moving slowly.*

ELLIOT: I saw her in pain . . . (*He stops by a door.*) Is this the bathroom I can see from my house? (*He pushes open the door, the bathroom is empty.*) I saw her right there . . .

They move further along the passage. Hearing a noise, CHARLOTTE *appears in the doorway of the bedroom; she has started to dress and is in her bra and panties. She is startled to see the two men coming down the passage, looking into every room, as if hunting for her.*

CHARLOTTE: What are you two doing?

ELLIOT: Are you feeling all right? I saw you through the window . . .

CHARLOTTE *is furious at the two of them creeping along the passage to see her.*

CHARLOTTE: You did, did you?! I knew you spied on us! Jesus, I knew that's what you were up to –

ELLIOT (*very startled*): I don't spy on you! . . . I just happened to see you through the window, you were unwell and –

CHARLOTTE: You just happened 'to see me'?!

ELLIOT *is so shocked by her hostility, he smiles nervously.*

ELLIOT: Yes . . .

CHARLOTTE: Is that why you're smiling then?

ELLIOT: I'm not smiling –

CHARLOTTE (*her voice rising*): I'm sorry, but don't you think it's pathetic – truly pathetic?!

ELLIOT: What? –

CHARLOTTE *is really upset, almost hysterical.*

CHARLOTTE: Letting people use this house – so you can stare at them through the window. You're just a fucking voyeur, aren't you? Watching everything from across the road . . . I knew this was what you are doing! Richard said, no, no, he's just an eccentric guy, but I saw you gazing at us, staring out of the window all the time –

ELLIOT: I never watch from across the road. Not on purpose. I did not –

CHARLOTTE: Christ, that's sad, isn't it?! That's really, really *sad*. Using other people's lives like that! Just because you can't even get out of the front door yourself! Can't do anything! Can't do anything with this house! Can't do anything with your life! No doubt you've seen me in the bathroom many times . . . hundreds of times probably! Taken pictures, have you?!

ELLIOT: I never, ever saw you in the bathroom before . . .

CHARLOTTE *suddenly sees* JOE's *shocked face watching all this.*

CHARLOTTE: And look what you've done to the boy. Just look at him . . . (JOE's *pale face.*) Getting him to watch too – Jesus, that's so sick! It's unforgivable! . . . You should be so ashamed of yourself . . .

Close-up of ELLIOT's *stunned face.*

INT. HALL. DAY
A crane shot moving down into the hall from high above the staircase. The hall is completely empty except for JOE *sitting cross-legged in the middle of the floor.*

JOE (*voice-over*): I know she got a shock, seeing us in the passage like that. I know she was angry with herself probably as well . . . But I haven't seen her since. The house seems very quiet. And Mr Graham doesn't visit. I see him through the window, once or twice . . .
We see ELLIOT *getting into his car outside his house. He smiles politely to the chauffeur.*

JOE (*voice-over*): And he looks OK, really.
We stay on ELLIOT *sitting in the shadows in the back of his car.*

JOE (*voice-over*): He's waiting for the results of Tina's work. Like he said to me in the cinema . . . everything will start to go forward then . . .

INT. MRS HOPKINS' OFFICE. DAY
MRS HOPKINS *standing in her little office, facing* JOE.

JOE (*voice-over*): Two things happened today. Mrs Hopkins told me she's leaving . . . She even gave me her keys.

MRS HOPKINS: It's time for me to move on, Joe, at last.

JOE: Right. (*Quiet.*) So you're moving on . . .

MRS HOPKINS (*looking at his pale face*): Are you OK?

JOE: I'm fine . . . (*He picks up her keys.*)

MRS HOPKINS: Not sure you should stay too long in this house, Joe . . .
But JOE *is holding both bunches of keys, sorting through them, studying them.*

JOE (*voice-over*): And then I heard Tina's finished her work.
She called me. We're going to hear the results on
Thursday.

INT. KITCHEN. DAY
We see ELLIOT *sitting at the kitchen table in the kitchen of the
big house.* JOE *is buttering some toast for all of them.* TINA *is
standing with her back to the sink, facing them, papers spread
out around her.*

ELLIOT: I like the idea of doing it here in the kitchen,
don't you, Joe? Less formal. (*Smiles.*) Easier for
everyone . . . to hear whatever it is.
TINA: So I think I've found something, Mr Graham.
Something new. Information that wasn't in anybody
else's report. And I think the best way . . .
ELLIOT *looks up from the kitchen table, obviously
nervous, moving things on the table.*
ELLIOT: Now just before we start, Tina, can you give me
an idea – this may not be very fair to ask, but on a
scale of one to ten, how bad is it?
He stares at TINA.
TINA: Not sure I can do that, Mr Graham. I mean, people
may take different attitudes to this, depending on who
they are. I mean, he wasn't the only one to do this –
ELLIOT: I don't like the sound of that!
Flashback. We see ELLIOT*'s father's face turning towards
us – sharp, fine features, a very pleasant smile – right into
the camera. He is peering at us from the very same
kitchen.*
YOUNG MR GRAHAM: Come here, tell me all about it.
We cut back to ELLIOT*'s eyes thinking about his father.
Then he looks up at* TINA.

ELLIOT: It's from the 1930s, isn't it? When he was very
    young, very inexperienced? I always thought there was
    something about how he got his start. Is it very bad?

TINA: There's no crime or anything – like it's not something
    he could have gone to jail for . . . Ready?

    ELLIOT *straightens.*

TINA: It was in a bunch of letters and loose diary pages,
    bundled together in a file called 'Country Walks'. I
    think that's why nobody else bothered to look at it . . .
    So shall I read you what he said? (*She reaches for the
    pages.*)

ELLIOT: No, I mean . . . not right this minute –

TINA: I think you should hear this, Mr Graham.

ELLIOT (*gripping the side of the table*): Of course I should.
    I just . . .

TINA: You want to know, don't you?

ELLIOT: Yes. (*He suddenly gets up.*) I do want to know . . .
    but I don't think I want to do this here, not now . . .
    I've changed my mind . . . There's something wrong
    about doing it in this house . . . I'm not putting it
    off . . . I'm not! Come with me, Tina! . . . Joe, you stay
    here. Got to get back to my house . . . We will do it . . .
    but . . .

    ELLIOT *leaves the room rapidly.* JOE *watches him
    disappear.*

INT. JOE'S ROOM IN THE LARGE HOUSE. AFTERNOON

JOE *is in his room in the large house, looking in a mirror. He
has become even paler. He is putting some sun-protection cream
on, smearing it on his lips and below his eyes, like sportsmen do.
It looks like warpaint.*

JOE (*voice-over*): Time to brighten myself up . . .

*We see him with the cream on his face, wandering through
the large, empty, shadowy ballroom. We see him staring at
the line of old shoes with the cream round his eyes.*

Two weeks have gone . . . since I saw them. I think
she must have told him.

We see a shot of ELLIOT *staring out of a window in his
house. Totally impassive, as if hiding in the shadows.*

JOE (*voice-over*): I only see him through the window . . .
I keep watching though . . . to see if I can catch him
in the street.

EXT. STREET. DAY

ELLIOT, *in a fine suit as if dressed for an important meeting,
is getting into the back of his car.*

Suddenly JOE *erupts from the door of the big house and
rushes across the street. He bangs on the car window.*

ELLIOT: Yes, Joe?

JOE: Just wanted to say hello and see how you were.

ELLIOT: I'm fine. I'm just off on a little trip to the country.

JOE: To the castle? You going to that castle you showed me
a picture of?

ELLIOT (*very startled*): As it happens, yes.

JOE: Can I come?

ELLIOT: No, Joe.

JOE (*pushing his head through the window*): Please can I come?

EXT. CASTLE. DAY

*We approach the castle. A fine medieval building with a moat,
nestling in rolling fields and surrounded by sheep. The moat is
full of water, lilies scatter the surface.*

We first see the castle through the window of ELLIOT's *car,
travelling shots, as we get closer and closer.*

JOE *is sitting on the back seat with* ELLIOT, *looking rather excited.*

The car stops. They get out in silence. ELLIOT *seems very preoccupied. He begins to move off towards the castle at once, and then stops, turns back for a moment, and nods at the chauffeur.*

ELLIOT: Thank you, Simon.

JOE *and* ELLIOT *begin to move towards the castle, past a little man selling tickets at the gate.* ELLIOT *nods silently at the man and the man nods back.*

There is nobody else around looking at the castle in the winter light. The trees are full of rooks and crows wheeling about.

ELLIOT *is moving slightly ahead of* JOE, *as if he has to reach somewhere quickly. He is talking in a sharp, staccato way.* JOE *has to run to keep up.*

ELLIOT: My father bought me this castle, Joe . . .

JOE: Bought it for you?!

ELLIOT: Yes, a birthday present. When I was nine. One of the few ways he communicated with me was by giving me presents. And this time he wanted to give me something I really, really wanted . . . and of course it seemed wonderful. What boy in the world had a greater present from their father . . . ! (*Then intensely to himself.*) And what could be wrong with such a gift? *They are moving towards the castle at a brisk pace. Suddenly out of the corner of his eye,* JOE *sees* ELLIOT'*s car disappearing away from them down the road that brought them to the castle. A moment later it has gone.*

JOE *turns and has to rush to catch up with* ELLIOT, *who is walking very purposefully.*

ELLIOT: It was round here I had my farm – a couple of miles over there – where I was happy. A dairy farm, a lovely place . . . I gave the castle to the National Trust . . . anybody can see it now. (*He stares around him.*) Not many of them here today, though! (*He is walking so rapidly he slips on the grass and has to steady himself.*) Not really dressed for this, am I?

JOE *suddenly is struck by the oddness of* ELLIOT *wearing his immaculate suit in the middle of a field in the country.*

JOE: You going to a meeting here?

ELLIOT: No, Joe.

They reach the water's edge near a bend in the moat, where there are some overhanging trees.

I'm looking for something, Joe . . . should be about here –

They come upon a large canoe tied up underneath the overhanging tree. It is covered in a blue tarpaulin.

I thought this might still be here . . . (*He begins tugging at the tarpaulin in a very determined fashion.*) I used to do this as a child . . . go round the castle in this . . . with my father. (*He is pulling hard at the tarpaulin.*) You don't mind going for a little ride in it? I think it is going to be a lovely afternoon.

We cut to JOE *in the front of the canoe paddling slightly awkwardly.*

ELLIOT *is sitting in the back of the canoe, holding himself very straight in his business suit. At first he is paddling too, but when they are out in the middle of the moat he stops, so the canoe moves at quite a stately pace through the water.*

You don't mind doing the driving, do you, Joe?

JOE: Not sure we'll go very quick. Only done this once before . . .

For a moment JOE *paddles, his face full of concentration.* ELLIOT *sitting gravely still behind him. The canoe moving through the dark water of the castle's moat.*

ELLIOT: That's very good, Joe . . . (*His face is full of quiet sorrow.*) Did Tina tell you what she found out about my father . . . ?

JOE: No, no, she didn't. Was it something before the Second World War like you said?

ELLIOT: Yes. You know, it wasn't difficult to guess it might be collaboration – doing business with the Nazis. I always thought there was a chance . . . My father as a very young man, he was based in America but worked here and in Europe too – he was very internationalist even then – always thought there was a small chance he made a lot of his early money doing business with the Germans. I hoped against hope it wasn't going to be really bad.   I mean, there were lots of people making money out of the Third Reich . . . Rockefeller in the US, of course, people getting them oil, getting them money. In this country too, of course . . . (*He stares at the castle as they drift past it.*) I mean, it's terrible of course. Unforgivable – but so many did it and some of their outfits are still going strong and doing very nicely, thank you . . .

We are on ELLIOT*'s face, the real pain and sorrow in his eyes.*

But there's something in my father's country walk . . .

FLASHBACK. EXT. A LARGE PARK. DAY

We are moving through a large park in the 1930s, seen through the window of a car, a travelling shot. We pass one or two faces sitting on benches, Berliners out in the sun.

The car is driving along one of the broad avenues in the park, a couple of people promenading the park stare into the car as it brushes past them, their faces very close.

We intercut between the park and ELLIOT *and* JOE *in the canoe as they move through the water of the moat.*

ELLIOT: It wasn't a country walk, as it happens. It was in a park (*slight laugh*) – literally 'a walk in the park' – only a walk in the park! In Berlin. In the late thirties. They drove to the park. There was a little party of them.

We see his father laughing in the car with four other young men in summer suits.

We then see travelling shots from the car. His father looks out of the window and sees a group of men in uniform moving towards a family picnicking under the trees. He points this out to his friends.

He was with some buddies – a couple from the British consulate, his American business colleague, and their German contact, who they were doing business with . . .

We are close on ELLIOT's *eyes.*

And what do they see?

The travelling shot of the men in uniform rounding up people in the park; at first we see it from a distance and it is difficult to work out exactly what is happening.

I can imagine it so easily, Joe, from what he wrote . . . First they see it from the car, while they are riding along . . . and it's difficult to work out what's going on . . . And then they get out of the car, Joe, and they think they will have a little look . . .

We move with the group of five young men towards the trees.

And then they see the storm troopers or police – he just describes them as young men in uniform – and they are stopping anybody who is Jewish, and they divide the men from the women.

We see them doing this to a huddle of about fifteen people.

And they make the men undress, right there in front of everybody on a Sunday afternoon . . . in the park.

We see six Jewish men, totally naked, being forced to crawl on all fours like dogs along the main path in the park.

The camera is moving with them, so we are on their level as they crawl along, with the uniformed men screaming at them, telling them to go quicker. And we see, from their level, the faces of women with their children staring at them from park benches and clapping. One of the mothers holds her golden-haired child up so he can get a better look.

And my father says simply, 'And the men were made to make quite an exhibition of themselves.' And then the women . . .

The camera moves towards the trees.

My father says, 'For the women, they had something straight out of the circus . . . '

We cut back to the canoe, JOE *paddling slowly, listening to* ELLIOT *with deep concentration.*

We intercut between ELLIOT*'s face of extraordinary pain and his father, with his young friends watching everything in the park with detached curiosity.*

They get close to the trees.

ELLIOT: It's not horror or anything . . . not bodies . . . but in a way it's almost worse . . .

The camera gets to the line of trees. We see there are long ladders leaning against the tall trees and the Jewish women are being made to climb the ladders. Some of the women are very old, one is only a child of twelve.

They made them climb the trees . . . the women were terrified . . . and then they took all the ladders away. And they were screaming at them, 'We want you to make a noise like a lot of birds . . . you are going to sing like birds . . . you are going to say cuckoo, cuckoo, you are going to sing tweet-tweet! SING!'

We see ELLIOT*'s father staring up, with a look of idle curiosity on his face as the women, totally traumatised, are sitting, holding on desperately to the branches, making pathetic noises, trying to sound like birds.*

ELLIOT: They had to chirp like birds or they were beaten
senseless . . . And you know what my father says? (*His
face full of anger now.*) The words my father uses . . .
what he said about what he and his business colleagues
saw in the park? . . . What he watched happen with two
men from the British consulate and the American?
*We see the group of men in uniform laughing together,
having a smoke, standing with a pile of ladders now lying
in the grass. They call up at the women in the trees, yelling
at them in German, 'Sing! Sing louder . . . You don't
sound like birds! Sing like birds!'*

*And we see a small cluster of Berliners staring up at the
trees with amused looks as the Jewish women are forced to
lift their heads and squeak from the branches.*

And we see ELLIOT's *father, staring up, rather intrigued.*

ELLIOT: He says . . . 'They certainly do things differently
here.' That's what he says . . . (ELLIOT's *eyes full of
fury.*) 'We all agreed' – I love that – 'We all agreed,
**THEY CERTAINLY REALLY DO THINGS
DIFFERENTLY HERE.**' It's the most terrible
sentence I've ever read, I think . . . These were the
people he was doing business with, that he was to owe
his fortune to . . .
We stay on ELLIOT's *face. The shock and pain.* JOE *looks
at him over his shoulder.* JOE *is very moved.*

ELLIOT: That's what Tina found.
We suddenly see the power in his eyes, a tremendous anger.
I was full of rage, Joe . . . these last weeks, full of rage
about what my father did . . . And then there were the
little animals . . . the ones you took on the telly . . .
*We see the animals in the hands of his father as he places
them on a shelf in one of the reception rooms of the large
house.*
They sat for years in the big house on a mantelpiece,
I remember being fascinated by them as a child . . .

and of course they had originally belonged to a Jewish family, they were stolen from them, given to my father as a present by his Nazi business colleagues. Did he know they were stolen? He knew what was going on – it doesn't really matter.

They have travelled along half the stretch of the moat. His tone suddenly changes.

Just let me off here, Joe . . . just here!

JOE (*surprised*): Here?

ELLIOT: Yes . . . Just want to take a stroll on my own . . . having relived all that . . . Just here will be fine!

We cut to ELLIOT on the bank, JOE still in the canoe.

ELLIOT: Joe, you couldn't be really kind now and take the canoe back? Just keep going round the moat that way . . . till you get to the place where we found it. Thank you. Most kind.

JOE: You'll meet me there?

ELLIOT: Oh yes . . . I'll meet you there.

JOE begins to continue to paddle round the moat. He cannot travel fast, and he is conscious that ELLIOT is moving quite briskly on the bank.

JOE suddenly hears a click and looks up. He sees ELLIOT is heading along the bank towards the trees holding a gun. He is holding the gun purposefully, in such a way that suggests he is used to handling firearms.

ELLIOT is walking fast through the thistles on the bank towards the mouth of the wood.

JOE yells out at him.

JOE: MR GRAHAM!

But ELLIOT is too far away, and the sound does not travel across the moat.

JOE paddles furiously towards the bank, trying to reach ELLIOT. He cannot move the big canoe fast enough and ELLIOT seems to be getting further and further away.

Eventually JOE *gets to the bank, he leaps out of the canoe, stumbling onto the bank, leaving the boat to drift back into the middle of the moat.*

He runs as fast as he can towards ELLIOT, *shouting.*

JOE: What are you doing?! Stop! STOP!

Then he turns and screams over his shoulder, back towards the gate.

Somebody help me . . . He's going to hurt himself!

JOE *rushes forward, nearing* ELLIOT. ELLIOT *turns with the gun; he looks quite frightening.*

ELLIOT: Keep away from me, Joe!

JOE: You can't do that! (*Shouting.*) You mustn't do that! . . . WHAT'S THE POINT OF DOING THAT?!

ELLIOT: I should never have brought you here. It was unforgivable of me to let you come with me. To involve you. Leave me, Joe . . . Please leave me.

JOE *continues to move towards him.* ELLIOT *is standing very straight.*

ELLIOT: You shouldn't be here, Joe . . . !

JOE: But I am . . . You brought me so I could stop you.

ELLIOT: That's not the case, Joe . . .

ELLIOT *stands very dignified in his business suit in the mouth of the wood. He lifts the gun to his head.*

JOE: NO!

JOE *hurls himself forward. He charges in a straight line towards* ELLIOT *with great force, trying to hurl his body against him.*

There is a loud crashing sound, not a bang, but a deep powerful sound.

The screen goes black as we hear the rooks shrieking. We fade up a moment later. The birds are swirling above the trees around the castle.

JOE *and* ELLIOT *are lying on the grass, about ten feet apart, in the shadow of the castle wall.* JOE *looks across* at ELLIOT. *He is lying on his back, watching the birds swooping above the castle. They lie for a moment in silence.* ELLIOT *glances at* JOE *and then back at the birds as they fly about in the winter light.*

ELLIOT: Quite right, Joe . . .

JOE *looks at him.*

ELLIOT: Quite right . . . (*His voice is very quiet.*) What was the point of doing that?

JOE: Yes . . .

ELLIOT (*very quiet*): Didn't dress for lying on the grass, did I?

JOE: No . . .

He sees the sadness in ELLIOT'*s eyes.*

JOE: Now you've found out everything . . . it will be different, remember?

ELLIOT: Will it? (*Quiet smile.*) Not sure I can make amends, Joe . . .

The sound of the wind and the birds.

JOE: You can meet new people . . . start going out again.

ELLIOT: That I can. You're right again, Joe. That I should do . . .

JOE: Both of us can . . . and not just to the deli and the lobster restaurant . . .

This makes ELLIOT *smile.*

ELLIOT (*quiet*): Yes. Of course. You're right.

JOE: What your father did, it was a difficult thing to find out, you needed to be a bit brave, like you said, to keep at it . . . And I think you were.

ELLIOT: Brave?! . . . Me?

JOE *glances across at him.*

JOE: I think so . . . yeah.

ELLIOT (*smiles*): Thank you, Joe . . .

They keep lying at the foot of the castle wall.

What about the house? Why didn't I do more with the house all these years? (*He turns and stares at* JOE.)

It wasn't particularly strong-minded of me to leave
the big house empty all that time, was it, Joe? To let
Richard and Charlotte use it . . . ?

JOE: That was OK. Letting them use it. What was wrong
with that?

ELLIOT: Maybe nothing . . . (*He watches the birds.*) Didn't
make them happy, though.

JOE *and* ELLIOT *continue to lie on the grass at the foot of
the castle battlements, staring upwards for a moment.*

We cut to JOE *and* ELLIOT *walking together, side by
side in the winter light, away from the castle.*

*The sound of the rooks circling and wheeling overhead
suddenly turns abruptly into the roar of London traffic.*

EXT. LONDON STREET. DAY

JOE (*voice-over*): I did see Richard again, just once . . . I was walking along, he suddenly yelled at me . . .
We see RICHARD *in his ministerial car, shouting out of the back window.*

RICHARD: Joe! Over here! Joe!
JOE *approaches the car. A young, attractive female adviser is sitting on the back seat with* RICHARD.

RICHARD: How are you? You look great!

JOE: I'm fine . . . (*Glancing at the woman, then back at* RICHARD.) And how are you?

RICHARD: Busy! Of course. We're fantastically busy, lots to implement! (*Then with a knowing smile straight at* JOE.) And I'm surviving too, as always! No, it's all great! (*As the car moves off, he calls back.*) See you again, Joe, sooner than you think . . .

JOE (*voice-over*): He always has to stay moving, like he said. I think he is scared of doing anything else. He never wants to be still for a single moment. Not sure where it gets him though.
We stay on RICHARD *for a moment, on the back seat of the car, the shot close to his face.*

EXT. RAILINGS. LEAFY STREET. DAY
We cut to a tracking shot along some railings. CHARLOTTE *and* JOE *are walking together on the edge of a leafy garden square.*

JOE (*voice-over*): I saw her too . . . We arranged to have a walk.
We see CHARLOTTE *in a dark dress walking close to* JOE.

JOE (*voice-over*): She told me about her kids. I told her about what Tina found.
We cut to CHARLOTTE.

CHARLOTTE: I always knew there was something sad about
that house, Joe . . . Maybe it was just me, of course,
what I was feeling, and I didn't really notice anything –
or maybe it is that place . . . (*She turns.*) You ought to
get out of there . . . out of that house, Joe.

JOE: I will . . . Yes. Soon.

CHARLOTTE: Not soon. Right now! You've got to get on
with your life, Joe.

JOE *is unconvinced.*

JOE: Yeah . . .

CHARLOTTE (*softly, touching his arm*): You should listen to
me. I care about you . . .

JOE *nods.*

CHARLOTTE: You know, Joe, it must have been awful for
Mr Graham to find out about his father, but in a way
I envy him.

JOE: Envy him?

CHARLOTTE: Yes . . . not for his money . . . (*She smiles.*)
Although I wouldn't say no to that . . . a little corner
of that! I mean, now he has found things out . . .
maybe it's solved his loneliness. (*She looks at him.*) I
can't do that, Joe. (*Their eyes meet.*) I can't do that . . .

INT. THE LARGE HOUSE. DAY
*We cut to a large-scale camera movement, tracking through the
front door of the big house, right across the hall, down passages,
and into the garden. The shot travels the entire length of the
house.*

*At the beginning of the shot we see dust and workmen in the
hall, dust sheets covering the marble floor, scaffolding up, the
beginning of the redecoration process of the house.*

*We move through the dust and turn down one of the long
passages.*

JOE (*voice-over*): The house is going to be totally redecorated
and changed . . . It'll still have a bit of a weird
atmosphere, I think, whatever colour they paint it . . .
It probably always will have.

We keep heading down the long passage.

Mr Graham is full of schemes and projects now –
things are going on all over the world . . . He's begun
to spend his money . . . And he's also searched very
hard and managed to find some relatives of the family
that owned the little animals . . . and they have been
returned to them – and are now sitting in a small
apartment in North Carolina.

The camera turns another corner in the passage.

And I've taken Charlotte's advice. I am leaving the
house. I need to do something different. I don't know
what yet. I am still thinking about it . . .

The camera comes out in the little garden. ELLIOT, TINA
and JOE *are sitting together in the sun, eating. They are
surrounded by produce from the deli and are gradually
working their way through it. They are eating calmly and
peacefully in the courtyard.* JOE *looks across at* ELLIOT.

JOE (*voice-over*): I'm proud of one thing, though. Tina
and I . . . we did stop him being stuck. He managed
some of that himself, and we did some of it too . . .

We stay on ELLIOT's *face, as he sits with* TINA *and* JOE.
ELLIOT *looks across at* JOE.

JOE (*voice-over*): So when we've finished this meal, but not
before, we are going to move on.

We see a high shot of ELLIOT, TINA *and* JOE *in the
courtyard, eating together.*

Fade to black.

CAPTURING MARY

Capturing Mary was produced by TalkbackTHAMES for BBC Television and HBO Films and was first screened in November 2007. The cast was as follows:

Mary	Maggie Smith
Joe Dix	Danny Lee Wynter
Young Mary	Ruth Wilson
Greville White	David Walliams
Liza	Gemma Arterton
Zach	Michael Byers
Mr Graham	Max Dowler
Musician	Jack Berkeley
Singers	Rebecca Bottone
	Claire Turner
	Celena Bridge

Writer/Director Stephen Poliakoff
Producer Deb Jones
Music Adrian Johnston
Director of Photography Danny Cohen
Film Editors Clare Douglas, Tom Kinnersley
Production Designer Mark Leese

INT. THE LARGE HOUSE. DAY

Credit sequence.

*The camera is moving at floor level along a passage in a
very large house. It pauses at an open doorway, glancing for a
moment into a room which has its curtains drawn and the
shutters closed against the light.*

*The camera moves on, sliding into a room full of a line of
old shoes from the fifties and sixties. The shoes are arranged in
neat rows.*

*We track along the shoes, both male and female footwear,
a line of past fashion. All of the shoes are expensive.*

*We dissolve as the camera probes deeper into the building,
past an umbrella stand full of old walking sticks and elderly
umbrellas. We take in a noticeboard in the kitchen with a menu
pinned up from a long-forgotten dinner party. We skim past
pictures from old magazines and newspapers from the fifties
and sixties. The whole building seems a time warp, as if very
little of the last thirty or forty years has penetrated it.*

*As the camera explores the empty house, we hear on the
soundtrack a seventeen-year-old boy with a south London accent.*

JOE (*voice-over*): I've been working for most of the year
in this big house in London. I'm on the door . . . It
belongs to Elliot Graham . . . who in the list of the
richest people in Britain was number eight.
*The camera begins to climb the fine eighteenth-century
staircase. It peers down for a moment at the mosaic floor
in the stairwell with its faded pattern of flowers.*
Nobody lives here now . . . Mr Graham himself lives
across the street in number 36 . . . all that happens in
this house is that it's cleaned every day . . . and people
arrange flowers here . . . there is always fresh flowers!
And then . . . when the cleaners all leave . . . I am
alone here – from between six and nine, I am by

myself . . . until the security guard turns up. I have this whole place to myself – every day!

The camera has climbed the stairs; in the distance it can now see a chunky boy of seventeen, JOE, *sitting cross-legged on the floor in the passage, listening to his Discman. The camera gradually skims up the staircase towards him.*

I am not allowed to let anybody in . . . not permitted to open the front door to any stranger. I never break this rule, ever. Not without Mr Graham's personal permission.

We have now reached JOE. *He glances up.*

But yesterday I did break it. The house shouldn't have been empty then – it was only ten to three – but the cleaners had left early.

He takes off his headphones and looks towards us down the passage.

End of credit sequence.

EXT./INT. THE FRONT DOOR OF THE LARGE HOUSE.
AFTERNOON

The front door of the big house has a panel that slides back, so you can talk to whoever is calling without opening the door.

JOE (*voice-over*): I really don't know why I broke the rule.

There is a sharp cut as the panel slides back to reveal an elegant-looking woman in her early seventies. She stares straight at JOE.

It was just something about her . . .

The woman, MARY, *smiles.*

JOE: Yes?

MARY: Is Mrs Hopkins in?

JOE: She doesn't work here any more.

MARY: Right. I see. (*She hesitates for a moment.*) I spoke to her on the phone a little while ago, and she was kind enough to say if I was passing and would like to look inside – I should just ring the bell. And today I was passing . . .

JOE: She stopped working here two weeks ago.

MARY (*pleasant smile*): Well, I'll go then.

Their eyes meet. MARY *doesn't seem to want to move.*

JOE: I can let you in, though.

MARY: Can you?

JOE: Please come in.

MARY: Thank you.

INT. THE LARGE HOUSE. LATE AFTERNOON

We cut to MARY *entering the big hall of the house. She is wearing a beautiful winter coat and her whole appearance is seemingly poised and immaculate. But at the same time she seems cautious, as if by crossing the threshold she is entering a potentially dangerous place.*

MARY: Thank you.

She stands stock-still for a moment in the middle of the imposing hall, with its pillars, its grand staircase and its faded mosaic floor. She suddenly cries out in surprise.

That door! It really is extraordinary, isn't it? I had forgotten how extraordinary it was!

At the side of the hall there is a substantial ornamental door. It is covered in black classical figures twisting and turning, writhing all the way up the door in many different poses. She smiles.

It seems even stranger than I remember it.

JOE: Yeah . . . it is strange. You get used to it, though.

MARY *is standing in the shadow in the hall.*

JOE: Was there . . . something you wanted to see specially? I mean, apart from the door?

MARY (*almost too quickly*): No, no, there is nothing.

Nothing I need to see . . . (*She smiles pleasantly, trying to sound offhand.*) I was just passing as I said, and I thought it would be fascinating to see inside . . . after all this time. For a moment. (*She turns.*) Just looking up an old haunt . . . I used to come here when I was young.

JOE: OK . . .

MARY *looks at* JOE.

MARY: I was almost as young as you.

JOE: Right.

JOE *watches her; again he has the impression she is nervous. Despite her elegant appearance, there is something about her manner; it is almost as if she is frightened of something.*

JOE: Well, I've got all the keys here . . . (*He lifts up his bulky cluster of keys.*) So if you change your mind, I can show you whatever you want . . . (*He rattles his keys and smiles.*) There's lots to see!

MARY: No, no, that won't be necessary! I don't want to cause any bother.

JOE: It's no bother. I like showing people the house. (*He smiles.*) Don't get many visitors . . .

MARY: No, being here in the hall is just fine. And I have another appointment very soon, anyway. I can't be here long.

JOE: It won't take long.

MARY (*very firmly*): No! I don't want to see the rest of the house!

Then she smiles, realising this must sound strange. JOE *is staring at her.*

MARY (*slight laugh, trying to sound relaxed*): I didn't come prepared for a guided tour! That's what I mean . . . (*She moves.*) It's beautifully kept, I must say . . . fresh flowers and everything . . . ! (*She turns.*) My name is Mary, Mary Gilbert.

JOE: I'm Joe.

MARY: Hello, Joe.

JOE: Joe Dix.

MARY (*smiles*): Hello, Joe Dix . . .

> *There is a pause.* JOE *watching her.*

MARY: I'll just be here for a moment, Joe, and then I'll be gone. If you need to do anything, please feel free . . . (*She smiles.*) I promise I won't steal anything.

JOE: I don't need to do anything.

MARY: Right . . .

JOE: Shall I get you some tea? I can do it quickly. Very quickly, so you don't miss your appointment . . .

> MARY *hesitates, then smiles.*

MARY: That's very kind.

INT. KITCHEN. AFTERNOON

JOE *moves round the kitchen in a determined fashion.*

In a series of fast cuts we see him assemble a beautifully laden tray for tea. The best china, a very elegant and rather large milk jug, a big pile of amaretti sweets and a little pyramid of shortbread which comes out of a big tin.

He cuts a couple of flowers from the vase in the kitchen and then drops them onto the tray, creating a real splash of colour.

As he waits for the kettle to boil, an impulse makes him move out of the kitchen, and from the shadows he stares into the hall to see what MARY *is doing.*

She is sitting strangely, very still, her back straight, as if she is keeping vigil.

He watches her for a second, fascinated.

INT. HALL. AFTERNOON

We cut to MARY *sipping the tea. The tray is now arranged in front of her on a little table in the hall.*

MARY: Beautiful tea, Joe! Thank you so much. (*She undoes an amaretto sweet.*) And these are delicious.

JOE: Good.

MARY: I'll just drink this . . . and then I'll be gone. I have to get to my appointment . . .

JOE: OK. I'll be over here . . . don't worry about me.

He sits at his concierge desk at the side of the hall.

Just got to fill in a few things in this ledger . . . all the hours I've done this week.

JOE puts on his Discman headphones. He sits pretending to work on the ledger, but he is glancing up at MARY whenever he thinks she isn't watching him.

For a moment the only sound in the hall is the click-click-click of the Discman. We stay on MARY's face.

She stares at the figures, twisted together on the door.

We cut back to her eyes. She looks sideways into the large room off the hall, the curtains and the shutters shut, shafts of late-afternoon winter sunlight piercing through them.

Very faintly, we hear the sound of two women's voices singing. They are singing an aria from a baroque opera, either from Handel or Vivaldi. It is haunting and beautiful, but when we hear it at first it is hushed, as if heard from a great distance.

MARY's eyes look tense. She glances sideways again at the room next to the hall. The lighting inside the room now looks totally different. It is night in there, the sidelights are glowing, there is the sound of faint laughter and people's voices. There is cigarette smoke floating in the air and shadows playing on the walls.

The singing is getting louder. MARY is sitting very still; we are back on her eyes.

We cut to the camera moving towards the room with the shadows and the laughter: it is curling towards the door as the aria grows louder and more intense.

.

A ping-pong ball suddenly comes bouncing out of the room, rolling along the mosaic floor of the hall and making a lot of noise for such a small white ball. We then see inside the room a figure is knocking another ping-pong ball against the wall; the noise is getting louder and louder and mixing with the opera.

A second ball flies out of the room and bounces sharply, directly towards the camera. It flicks straight at the lens.

MARY *flinches as if she can see it in the present and it is about to hit her. But we cut wide to see* MARY *is still alone with* JOE *in the hall.* JOE *with his Discman headphones on.*

The camera moves directly towards MARY. *Suddenly it is intercut with a shot travelling down one of the passages in the house as the singing reaches a crescendo. We glimpse, a very long way from us, two young women singing the aria in fifties ball gowns.*

We move in on MARY's *face in the present as the aria gets louder and louder. There is real pain in her eyes, something darker than sorrow.*

We hear JOE's *voice cutting through the music, at first faintly and then really loudly. The aria stops abruptly in the middle of a phrase.*

JOE: Miss . . . ! MISS!

MARY *looks up. She has knocked over the substantial milk jug, and milk is pouring down the side of the tray onto the mosaic floor of the hall.*

MARY: I am so sorry! How clumsy of me . . .

JOE: It's OK! Wait there!

He has dashed out of the hall. He returns with a large bucket and mop.

This'll do it . . .

MARY: Let me –

JOE: No, no!

JOE *starts mopping the milk vigorously with the mop, which is rather too large for the task. He produces another cloth and kneels on the floor and begins to wipe the milk that way.*

MARY: You kindly let me in here . . . and I spill things over the beautiful floor . . . !

JOE: Don't worry . . . (*He grins.*) It's only milk!

As he moves on all fours across the mosaic floor wiping the milk, he suddenly looks up at MARY.

JOE: What happened here?

MARY: What do you mean?

JOE: Something happened to you here . . . I mean before. When you were young?

MARY: Is that what you think, Joe?

JOE: Yeah . . .

MARY: Just because I don't want to see the rest of the house doesn't mean something happened here.

But JOE refuses to be deflected.

JOE: Why did you used to come here?

There is the faint sound of a piano being played on the soundtrack.

MARY: I came as a guest . . .

JOE: To big parties?

MARY: No. (*She smiles.*) Quite small parties.

JOE: Small parties?

MARY: They were very select.

The sound of the piano is getting louder on the soundtrack. It was amazing this house then . . . I had never seen anything like it . . .

FLASHBACK. INT. HALL/RECEPTION ROOMS. NIGHT
Through the sequence we intercut between the night flashbacks and the present in winter sunlight.

We see the camera tracking along a rail of fur coats, magnificent women's coats of the late fifties, as MARY's voice continues.

MARY (*voice-over*): Mr Graham's father invited people here
he considered important. Once a week he had a little
soirée. So when you came here – there were few
guests, but nearly all of them were giants . . .
*The camera is peering into a half-empty room. We see a
cluster of men in dinner jackets in the distance; half
glimpsing them, the camera pushes around the back of
somebody who is blocking our view.*
Great novelists, famous people from the movies,
actors and directors, scientists, politicians of course,
too . . . those were the only guests. You would crane
your neck all the time – to try to get a glimpse.
*We see a small man disappearing down a passage, the
camera following him, trying not to run after him but
determined to get a better view.*
Was that really E. M. Forster that just walked past
you . . . ? Is that figure over there in the chair Alfred
Hitchcock? I think that's Ava Gardner there, deep in
the shadows, by that plant . . .
*We see a mysterious figure, half masked from us by the
leaves of a plant. We then move towards two men talking,
sitting with their backs to us.*
Is that the back of Evelyn Waugh's head . . . ?
*A face, half in shadow, wearing glasses, nods at us, as he
walks past the camera, moving in the other direction down
the passage.*
And was that T. S. Eliot who half said hello?
We cut back to the present.

MARY: You may have done some of those writers at school,
Joe?

JOE: No. Not sure I did. I'll look them up, though. (*He
stares straight at her.*) Why were you there?

MARY (*laughs*): How on earth did I get invited? That's a
very good question, Joe! Me, a very young woman

who'd only just lost her Manchester accent . . . You wouldn't have guessed that's where I came from, would you?

JOE *is confused by this question.*

JOE: Hadn't thought about it.

MARY: I forced myself to lose my accent at university. (*Self-mocking smile.*) Taught myself to speak like this . . .

FLASHBACK. INT. RECEPTION ROOM. NIGHT

We move around the shoulder of a large, bulky man in a dinner jacket to glimpse YOUNG MARY, *standing on her own, in the doorway of one of the large reception rooms. There is something confident and fearless about her as a young woman, a glint of humour in her eyes, as if she relishes observing the world and is amused by what she sees.*

During MARY's *voiceover we watch her younger self move slowly into the room, glimpse her between men's shoulders and clouds of cigarette smoke.*

MARY (*voice-over*): I was there because I had been very lucky and become rather well known in my own right. At Oxford I wrote a lot of journalism and one of my pieces got picked up by a Sunday newspaper. Suddenly I was writing about movies and culture . . . I did an interview with Cary Grant, and he very unexpectedly opened up to me and talked about his depression . . . the article caused something of a sensation – those sort of things weren't ever discussed then. This was a long time ago, Joe . . . You can't really imagine what the world was like then . . .

We cut to JOE *in the present, standing very still in the big empty hall staring straight at* MARY *and then we cut back to the past.*

We see the YOUNG MARY *sitting at the back of the room next to an older woman who is wearing a long evening dress, pearl necklace and white gloves.*

MARY (*voice-over*): We're talking right at the end of the fifties. It was a very class-bound time of course, full of absurd rules and ridiculous prejudices – even about how you use your fork at mealtimes.

We are now watching the YOUNG MARY *moving among the guests, watching everything, confident and poised.*

MARY (*voice-over*): Me attending these parties on my own – that was deemed very unusual.

We see men's faces turning to stare at the YOUNG MARY.

MARY (*voice-over*): A young woman, and I was very young, from the North sounding off in the press was a real novelty . . . Suddenly I had my own column . . . I wrote a book with a silly title, *Slicing the Apple*, that caused a stir – it was an attack on the male elite, in politics, in the arts, a bit of a tirade too against the butler-festooned world of British movies and television, and the BBC accent that was piped at you from every orifice then. The smell of Empire that still clung on . . .

We see YOUNG MARY *in wide shot sitting with a row of old people in evening dress, listening to the two young opera singers singing a glorious aria from the other end of the room.*

The camera floats closer to these older people, examining their immaculate dress, their formal clothes and manners, their sleepy satisfied faces.

We suddenly cut back to the present for a moment.

MARY (*laughs*): Nothing remarkable, of course, really, Joe! It was who was saying it that excited people . . . This was before the Beatles and all of that, of course.

JOE: Yeah . . . (*Thoughtfully.*) Before the Beatles . . .

MARY (*a self-mocking smile*): The confidence of youth . . . !

We cut to YOUNG MARY, *her sharp observant face. And as we hear the words of her column the camera plays across the faces of the audience listening to the opera in the main reception room of the house. We see the women's magnificent fifties dresses, their jewellery, and the men smoking cigars and looking relaxed and self-important.*

YOUNG MARY (*voice-over*): A month ago regular readers of this column will remember I advocated a little more passion in our native cinema, that perhaps physical love was not best expressed by a small peck on our jaunty hero's cheek by his long-suffering wife as he sets off for work in the morning, whistling.

I also ventured the thought that it was important that audiences were treated as adults and therefore sexual love was clearly a proper subject for cinema and that ultimately we might see some representation of the actual sexual act in mainstream pictures.

I have to admit I was anticipating a lot of letters, and indeed that is what I have received, most of them either accusing me of calling for the floodgates to be opened to pornographers or else that I had insulted our fine British acting fraternity by implying they were a trifle sexless.

We then cut back to MARY *with* JOE *in the empty hall.*

MARY: I wrote an article saying there should be far more sex in the movies. (*She laughs.*) All hell broke loose . . . !
We cut back to the past, the two young opera singers performing and YOUNG MARY *watching.*

MARY (*voice-over*): So there I was, Joe . . . sitting with these titanic figures . . . though I always kept to the back of the room. And I was thrilled to be there, I have to admit! Star spotting – I wasn't above a bit of that. And I kept being invited! And I felt really alive . . . buzzing with ideas and the possibility of things . . . !

We see MR GRAHAM, *a thin-faced, not particularly impressive-looking man, wandering absent-mindedly in and out of the room as the singers perform.*

MARY (*voice-over*): People wandered about and chatted as the singers sung . . . it was more like a rich man's background music. (*She smiles.*) Glorious muzak.

A sudden cut back to the present. The notes of the aria hang on and reverberate for a second around the empty house.

JOE is standing in the doorway of the room next to the hall.

JOE: Was it in here? The singing?

MARY: Partly in there . . .

JOE: Come and have a look at it now.

MARY: I don't need to do that.

JOE: Come on . . .

INT. LARGE RECEPTION ROOM. LATE AFTERNOON

MARY *enters the large room very reluctantly.* JOE *is struck by her demeanour, she seems really to have to brace herself to cross into the room, which is entirely empty, except for a few banqueting chairs stacked in an ugly pile.*

Another aria begins faintly – a ghostly sound, echoing around the empty room.

JOE *watches* MARY.

JOE: Did somebody die in here or something?

MARY: Why do you ask that?

JOE: Because you didn't want to come in.

MARY *stares across the room.*

MARY: It looks smaller . . .

She sits on the one banqueting chair that is not stacked. We move towards her, as the new aria gets louder.

We cut back to the past. The air is now really thick with cigarette and cigar smoke, and through the smog the two young girls continue to sing.

MARY (*voice-over*): The funny thing is . . .

The camera is searching through the smoke, the guests for a moment have become silhouettes.

The person I found most interesting was not one of the living legends – I found myself becoming really fascinated by this man who wasn't at all famous . . . in fact, nobody there was quite certain what he did. I noticed people seemed a little nervous of him as he approached . . . even Alfred Hitchcock! And then I began to understand why . . . when I managed to eavesdrop on what he was saying. He would whisper to these great writers and movie directors and actors, 'Your latest doesn't seem to have caused quite such a stir as the last one . . . It is still on, isn't it?'

Through the cigarette fog we see for the first time GREVILLE, *a very smart man in his thirties or forties. He has a charming smile, sharp, a little mercurial rather than warm. He moves round the room as the women sing, chattering to people, whispering close so as not to cause too much of a disturbance.*

We see the YOUNG MARY *watching him.*

GREVILLE (*indicating the opera singers as people applaud one of their arias*): Aren't they splendid! . . . He spots them in the chorus at the opera. (*Indicating* MR GRAHAM.) He has a great eye for talent . . . No, no, it's not a recent thing at all, he has always been good at that, ever since I have known him. I'd love to claim it is something to do with me, but it isn't.

We hear the older MARY's *voice as the camera follows* GREVILLE. *The camera getting closer and closer, trying to pick up what he is whispering.*

We get close to GREVILLE's *whispering and hear both* MARY *in the present and* GREVILLE *speaking in the past.* GREVILLE *moves to another guest.*

MARY (*voice-over*): 'Well, I liked it . . . I don't know why I am so alone . . . !'

GREVILLE: 'You must be so relieved! They seem to be going despite the notices!'

He moves on, to whisper to somebody else.

MARY (*voice-over*): He seemed to weave a web around these great figures . . .

GREVILLE: 'I think people are just a little confused, that's what I think . . . but it won't have done you any harm, will it . . . ?'

MARY (*voice-over*): A rather destabilising web – but he did it with such a charming smile, so somehow they were forced to take it . . .

We follow GREVILLE into the passage where he whispers to somebody else. This time we can't hear what he is saying.

MARY (*voice-over*): People said he was in 'publishing' . . . that as a very young man he had worked with Lloyd George on his papers, getting them in order, and now he was doing the same for Winston Churchill . . .

We move in on GREVILLE in the passage. Suddenly he is alone. He starts knocking a ping-pong ball about against the wall with a bat, initially gently and then more vigorously, as if getting rid of a great deal of pent-up energy.

MARY (*voice-over*): And he also helped all these old generals and admirals get their memoirs published after the war. He was very friendly with the great newspaper proprietors of the time, Beaverbrook and Rothermere . . . so he knew everybody that mattered! He was one of those mysterious people who seem to do both everything and nothing . . .

We see YOUNG MARY moving from her seat in the reception room to watch GREVILLE from the shadows hitting the ping-pong ball in the passage.

MARY (*voice-over*): Sometimes I would see him thrash this
ball about in the passage. It was a strange thing to do,
but nobody stopped him. I was getting increasingly
intrigued . . . people said he knew so many secrets,
but he never ever disclosed what he knew . . .
We see GREVILLE *turn in the passage. The* YOUNG MARY
*instinctively dodges back into the reception room, hoping
he hasn't seen her watching him.*

MARY (*voice-over*): The other extraordinary thing he did . . .
*The camera is now moving past two of the great ladies in
their evening dresses, sitting in the reception room listening
to the singing, to discover a beautiful young girl, no more
than a child of fifteen, but a very sexually confident-
looking child.*

MARY (*voice-over*): He brought these extremely young girls
with him – gorgeous young things . . . but definitely
underage.
We see GREVILLE *moving with a young girl* (LIZA)
around the room, introducing her to people.

MARY (*voice-over*): Every time there was a different girl . . .
On my fourth visit there was this particularly glorious
creature. I couldn't hear how he introduced her . . .
His niece? A friend of the family?
We see LIZA *moving with* GREVILLE. *He guides her
among the guests.*

LIZA (*to Alfred Hitchcock*): I thought that film – the one
that happened all in autumn, with those lovely
trees – I thought that was very jolly! It made me
laugh, no, it did! Was that a real dead body they
were dragging around . . . ? (*She laughs sweetly.*) No,
no, I realise that of course . . . that you're not allowed
to do that . . . but I thought you might have done it
all the same!
LIZA and GREVILLE *move round the guests together.*

LIZA (*to* MR GRAHAM): Do you keep any of your money
here? (*She smiles.*) No, I mean – do you have huge
safes . . . that have to be guarded – with dogs and
things – in case people come in . . . you know, trying
to safe-crack? Is that what it's called?! (*She laughs
merrily.*) Why is it 'cracking' . . . that's quite funny,
isn't it . . . ?! I would love to see one of your big safes.
(*She leans towards him.*) You don't have any . . . Well –
(*She smiles sweetly.*) I'm disappointed.

The YOUNG MARY *sits again as the aria rises and rises.
She is rather closer to the front now and nearer to where*
GREVILLE *is.*

MARY (*voice-over*): I had never spoken to him. Not yet.
Occasionally I would see him glance towards me, in a
slightly knowing way, as if to say, 'You and I . . . we're
both observers, aren't we?' And on this evening, my
fourth visit, he was getting closer and closer – would
he speak to me? As he got really near, I found myself
getting excited, more excited absurdly than if Alfred
Hitchcock has been coming to talk to me! And when
he got close . . .

We see GREVILLE *look sideways and give* YOUNG MARY
a particularly warm smile.

We cut back to the present. The empty stark room. JOE
watches MARY.

JOE: And what did he say?

We stay on MARY's *eyes for a second.*

FLASHBACK. INT. KITCHEN. NIGHT

*The camera moves down a passage in the past, and into the
large kitchen of the house. It is full of shiny pots and pans and
is spotlessly clean.* YOUNG MARY *is entering the kitchen.*

YOUNG MARY (*bumps into a maid*): Oh, sorry.

MARY (*voice-over*): I had just gone into the kitchen . . . to get myself a glass of water. It seemed absurd to ask a servant to do that. When suddenly . . .

GREVILLE *puts his face round the door.*

GREVILLE: I'm not disturbing you, am I?

YOUNG MARY: No, of course not.

GREVILLE: Both of us have escaped to the kitchen –

YOUNG MARY: I just came to get myself some water.

GREVILLE: Right . . . Well, as for me, I'm going to really shock you, I think . . .

YOUNG MARY (*remaining poised*): Are you? I doubt that.

GREVILLE (*smiles*): I've come here to make myself a salad . . .

YOUNG MARY *laughs.*

GREVILLE: I have. One of my little foibles when it gets late. The staff leave me the ingredients (*he indicates a line of vegetables and greens laid out next to the sink*) – and I make myself a salad. Does that shock you?

YOUNG MARY: Of course not.

GREVILLE (*merrily*): You're lying . . . It is a little eccentric, I admit.

YOUNG MARY: I haven't introduced myself, I'm –

GREVILLE: It is me who has to introduce himself! I'm Greville White. I know of course who you are, Mary Gilbert, because you are famous.

YOUNG MARY: Hardly!

GREVILLE: Absolutely. You are. I hang on your every word . . . I can quote whole paragraphs. (*He grins.*) Well, maybe not whole paragraphs . . . (*He moves towards the vegetables, rolling up his sleeves.*) You are an 'acid observer', isn't that right, slicing people down to size . . . ? (*He grins before she can reply.*) I do a bit of that too, I suppose . . . though of course I don't write it down. (*He glances up as he begins making the salad, slicing the vegetables vigorously.*) But I know a few things . . .

YOUNG MARY: I bet you do.

GREVILLE: 'The Voice of Youth.' Isn't that what it says, your byline in the newspaper? The true voice of youth . . . !

YOUNG MARY: That was awful. I stopped them doing it.

GREVILLE: What a fantastic opportunity that is, though, to be the voice of youth! (*He grins.*) I would grab it if I were you.

YOUNG MARY (*lightly*): I'm trying to . . .

For a moment GREVILLE *works at his salad.*

GREVILLE: You know, one thing I often do – well, often is a lie – one thing I occasionally do . . . is see myself as others see me. Quite vividly, in fact. Do you ever do that?

YOUNG MARY: No.

GREVILLE: You sure?

YOUNG MARY: I'm not certain what you mean –

GREVILLE: I'll tell you exactly what I mean . . .

He stops making the salad for a moment and looks at YOUNG MARY.

GREVILLE: When I think about myself, most of the time I see myself as dapper – (*He smiles.*) Wonderful word, 'dapper' . . . and maybe I've got a little more energy than some other people. You have that too, Mary. And maybe I've got a good memory, and a reasonably lively mind . . . that's how I see myself!

He suddenly sits in a chair opposite MARY.

GREVILLE: But sometimes I conjure up the picture other people have of me . . . what they see.

We cut back to MARY *in the present. Her face looks shocked, reliving the moment.*

MARY: And suddenly he seemed almost to change shape in front of my eyes. He seemed to be fatter, sweatier, older.

We cut back to the past in the kitchen. GREVILLE *has sprawled back in his chair, his face sweating, his hair messy, his tie loose, his cheeks slightly red.*

GREVILLE: They see me as quite a slimy, maybe treacherous fellow – sweaty . . . always with little beads of sweat on his brow, as if I'm working too hard trying to be charming, covering what's really going on inside and the effort shows . . . Whatever the temperature of the room, whatever the season, they see the sweat . . .

YOUNG MARY stares at the sprawled figure in the chair with true surprise. She is trying hard to remain unruffled.

We cut back to MARY in the present.

MARY: Never forgotten that . . . him slumped in the chair, staring at me, having conjured the sweat from somewhere . . . It was really startling . . .

We cut back to the past. GREVILLE *looks thoughtful, glancing at YOUNG MARY, as if now slightly embarrassed. Then he leaps up, back to his dapper self.*

GREVILLE (*charming smile*): Don't worry, a little party trick! Hopefully not too many people see me like that.

He looks at YOUNG MARY.

YOUNG MARY: I'm sure they don't.

GREVILLE (*grins*): Come on, no need to be bland with me, Mary Gilbert – that's not what you're famous for! I'm quite certain you for a start have viewed me like that – in fact, you have already tonight!

YOUNG MARY: I'm sure I haven't –

GREVILLE: Don't worry, I'm not offended. In the slightest.

YOUNG MARY: I can tell you, Mr White –

GREVILLE: Please, Greville –

YOUNG MARY: I don't know you. I know nothing about you, so I couldn't have thought those things about you –

GREVILLE: I promise you, I really promise you, I am not offended. And what's more I'm going to prove it to you. Now.

YOUNG MARY: Prove it to me?

GREVILLE: By doing something I never usually do – telling you a few little things that might amuse you (*smiles*) – since you are an observer yourself. I never gossip as a rule . . .

YOUNG MARY: I'd heard.

GREVILLE: Oh, so you do know something about me!

YOUNG MARY: I'd heard that.

GREVILLE: Yes, well, I never, ever gossip – too many useful things would be compromised if I did. But for you, young Mary Gilbert (*he smiles*) – I will make an exception. My only exception . . .

We move in on YOUNG MARY's *face as we hear* MARY's *voice in the present.*

MARY (*voice-over*): And so, as he put the finishing touches to his salad, he told me a few little titbits – a famous politician who was having an affair with a minor royal was perhaps the only juicy revelation . . . They were mostly mild harmless stories, like a civil servant who had an obsessive need to pick people's pockets.

We see GREVILLE *talking and smiling.*

GREVILLE: He slipped all sorts of things into his pockets, not just watches and wallets, but sometimes people's cough lozenges . . .

We cut back to MARY *in the present.*

MARY (*voice-over*): There was a funny story about a famous Hollywood star who came to make a movie in England. She was terrified of Pekinese dogs, regarded seeing them as a terrible omen – so if she caught sight of one from her car on the way to the film studios, she would refuse to film that day.

We cut to MARY *smiling in the present, and then back to* GREVILLE *and* YOUNG MARY *in the kitchen.*

MARY (*voice-over*): So the film company was reduced to hiring special dog-walkers, all with great big dogs, to amble along the streets near her hotel each time she set off in the morning.

GREVILLE: I met her once – apart from the business with dogs she was rather nice. She swore an awful lot. She had a charming Southern accent.

We cut back to MARY *in the present.*

MARY: It was fascinating being deluged with gossip as he made his healthy-looking salad . . . He was funny and charming. But I had no doubt as I sat there . . . as I watched him . . . I was under no illusion that, though I was quite well known then and nobody outside the elite circle knew who he was – here was somebody who was far more powerful than me, who could do me harm, who I had to be extremely careful of . . .

We cut back to YOUNG MARY *in the kitchen.*

YOUNG MARY: I suppose they are quite scary, Pekinese, if you don't like dogs, all that hair and those little faces –

GREVILLE: Talking of hair, there is a senior politician I know whose great thrill it is to cut other people's hair. He dresses up in a gentleman's barber's outfit –

YOUNG MARY (*laughs*): Oh, come on!

GREVILLE: No, this is true . . . He puts on a white apron, he has a special barber's chair in the front room in his house, he has lots of different scissors and clippers, and he does a jolly good haircut. I've had mine done by him more than once.

YOUNG MARY (*laughing*): Does he charge as well?

GREVILLE: No, no, quite the opposite. You get a glass of sherry and some cheese biscuits!

MARY (*voice-over, as we move in on* YOUNG MARY'*s face*): And I kept on asking myself, why is he telling me this? It's more than just trying to get me into bed? What is he really after?

We cut back to the present. JOE *is suddenly moving across the reception room, heading deeper into the house.*

MARY: Where are you going?

    JOE *turns in the door of the reception room.*

JOE: Going to see where it happened. Are you coming?

MARY: Do we have to?

    We cut back to the kitchen in the past. GREVILLE *turns
    and faces* YOUNG MARY *and thumps the great big salad
    down in front of her.*

GREVILLE: What do you think?

YOUNG MARY: It looks terrific.

INT. KITCHEN. LATE AFTERNOON

We cut to a light flicking on in the present. JOE *is standing in
the empty kitchen. The winter-afternoon light is just dipping
outside; it will soon be dusk.*

MARY is standing on the edge of the kitchen, not quite entering.

MARY: It's hardly changed! That's terrible. It's like it's been preserved. It should have changed more . . .

JOE: Yeah . . . It's really old-fashioned, I agree.

MARY: I don't like that at all – that it's hardly changed.
She looks across towards the sink. GREVILLE *turns to face her from the past, standing by the sink. We cut back to* MARY *flinching at the memory.*

JOE: Did you get to eat his salad?

MARY (*slight smile*): Funny you should ask that! I was just thinking that very second, I never got to taste it –

FLASHBACK. INT. KITCHEN. NIGHT
We cut back to the kitchen in the past. GREVILLE *and* YOUNG MARY *staring at the salad.*

GREVILLE (*grins*): It is beautiful, isn't it? You're right!

YOUNG MARY: Yes.

GREVILLE: Thank you.
We hear from far away the sounds of the singers beginning another aria.

GREVILLE: And it is just for us two.

YOUNG MARY: Just for us! We'll never finish it!

GREVILLE: Shall we go and choose some wine to go with it?
YOUNG MARY *hesitates, confused by this.*

YOUNG MARY (*indicating where the music is coming from*):
You mean go and get a glass from out there?

GREVILLE: No, I mean from the cellar.

YOUNG MARY: The cellar?

GREVILLE: Yes. I often do that. Mr Graham has a fantastic wine cellar, but I am not sure he knows his way round it – he frequently asks me for recommendations . . .

and he lets me take a bottle home when I wish . . .
One of my little perks.

He looks straight at YOUNG MARY.

GREVILLE: Do you want to come and help me choose?

YOUNG MARY *hesitates.*

GREVILLE: It's quite interesting down there . . . it's a very
old house . . .

MARY (*voice-over*): It was like a dare . . . For some reason
I had to follow him.

YOUNG MARY *is moving with* GREVILLE *down the long
central passage of the house.*

GREVILLE: You ever written about wine?

YOUNG MARY (*lightly*): No, I know absolutely nothing
about wine.

GREVILLE: So there are some things you don't have an
opinion on then?!

YOUNG MARY: Of course! There are all sorts of things
I don't know anything about – naturally!

GREVILLE: Really? I'm sure that can't be true, Mary.

YOUNG MARY: Well, it is. (*She laughs.*) I see myself very
much as a beginner still. I've been very lucky in my
career . . .

GREVILLE (*lightly*): But it's good to have strong opinions.
(*Warm smile.*) I approve of that.

MARY (*voice-over*): The house was full of famous people . . .
all around us . . . I felt safe . . .

*We move with them along the passage. Away from the
glowing reception rooms. The sound of the singing gets
fainter and fainter.*

I realised he was most probably trying to seduce me –
but I don't know why, I wasn't the least afraid of him.
I felt I could handle him . . . I knew he wasn't going
to try to rape me . . . And I knew instinctively there
was something else he wanted to tell me.

They turn a corner in the passage.

And of course a bit of me was thinking, maybe there's
a story here . . .

We cut to GREVILLE *opening a door leading to the
basement.*

MARY (*voice-over*): So we went down the stairs . . .

INT. CELLAR AND PASSAGES. NIGHT

*The camera is travelling down the subterranean passages of the
big house. The original brick walls of the eighteenth-century
cellars lit by little fifties lights. It is very dark, with big shadows.*

We see the YOUNG MARY *in her evening dress following*
GREVILLE *along the passages.*

MARY (*voice-over*): It was extraordinary being down there
 . . . but I could still hear the singing from upstairs . . .
 I didn't feel afraid.

*They turn a corner in the passage. It is even darker
ahead.*

MARY (*voice-over*): But I did of course think, what on earth
 am I doing following this man deeper and deeper into
 the cellars?

GREVILLE *turns and looks at* YOUNG MARY.

GREVILLE: Up until twenty years ago the food used to
 come along here from the kitchens. Can you believe
 that?

They continue moving along the passageways.

 I know it seems spooky down here – but it isn't.

He stops by a door.

 It is in fact rather beautiful.

YOUNG MARY: Beautiful? Maybe . . . in a way.

*He opens the door. There is the main wine cellar, with all
the bottles glowing in a slightly ghostly white light.*

GREVILLE: Isn't this magnificent?!

YOUNG MARY (*smiles*): Yes . . . it is.

GREVILLE *moves towards the bottles.*

GREVILLE: Some of these bottles are over a hundred years old. Mr Graham bought up other people's wine collections and stuck them down here. There are some real treasures, that are worth a fortune . . . (*He moves among the bottles.*) I persuaded him recently to do some better labelling . . . I wrote some of these myself.

They move past the rows of bottles.

YOUNG MARY (*smiles*): Great labels.

GREVILLE *turns.*

GREVILLE: Thanks. Yes, they are rather nice. (*He smiles at her.*) *You* know about films . . .

YOUNG MARY: Yes –

GREVILLE: Well, this a bit like something in the fat chap upstairs' movie. You know, *Notorious*, where they go down to the wine cellar. Cary Grant – and you don't know what he is going to discover – and then Ingrid Bergman joins him . . .

YOUNG MARY: I'm not sure we are going to find some uranium down here, in one of these bottles!

GREVILLE *turns.*

YOUNG MARY: That's what Cary Grant found.

GREVILLE: No. Maybe not . . . But here we have this –

He stops by a beautifully hand-painted label for 1900.

We have a Château Latour from 1900 – one of the greatest wines of the century.

He lovingly touches the bottle, taking it off the shelf.

And as they were drinking this, little did they know what a disaster was going to overcome them all . . . in a few years. (*He puts the bottle back.*) I like doing this – imagining what was happening as certain wines were bottled.

He moves round the corner into an even darker part of the cellar.

Château Haut-Brion – (*He smiles.*) Often described as a very feminine wine . . . 1929 was a truly great year.

YOUNG MARY (*touching the 1929 label*): Just as stock markets of the world were collapsing and people were throwing themselves out of buildings –

GREVILLE: Exactly . . . and then, come here . . . 1943 – the best vintage during the war! (*He smiles.*) The connoisseur's life very definitely didn't stop, you see . . .

YOUNG MARY: You do know a lot about wine.

GREVILLE: Well, I spend an awful amount of my time in country houses drinking this stuff . . . (*he smiles*) as I help them out . . . So I've acquired a little knowledge – about various things . . .

YOUNG MARY: I wouldn't complain if I were you. Nice way to spend your time.

GREVILLE *looks at her for a moment.*

GREVILLE: Was I complaining? I didn't mean to.

YOUNG MARY, *trying to defuse the moment, smiles at him.*

YOUNG MARY: Shall we choose a bottle then? Maybe the one that's worth a fortune – that would surprise them, if we went upstairs waving that around, having opened it!

GREVILLE's *tone suddenly changes.*

GREVILLE: I lied to you.

YOUNG MARY: About what? (*She stares at him, unafraid.*) The reason for us coming down here?

GREVILLE: No. (*He smiles, not offended.*) What do you take me for, Mary? I don't normally lure young women down into cellars to take advantage of them . . . (*He looks at her.*) No, I lied about the stories I told you.

YOUNG MARY: You mean they weren't true?

GREVILLE: No, they were true all right. But they were silly, unimportant, froth.

He is staring at her across the wine cellar.

They weren't the real story . . .

The camera moves round the YOUNG MARY.

GREVILLE: I should have been more truthful.

MARY (*voice-over*): As he said that, before he said anything else, I could feel myself go cold . . .

GREVILLE: Do you want to hear the real story, Mary?

YOUNG MARY (*very quiet*): How do you mean?

GREVILLE *stands still, his hand goes up to his forehead.*

MARY (*voice-over*): He looked at me almost in pity, as if he might be going to spare me something – like he had pity for both of us, and that we shouldn't have to have these images in our head. The images he was about to give me . . . And then he said – 'Do you want to hear that?'

We move in slowly on YOUNG MARY's *face. We cut back to* GREVILLE *watching her.* YOUNG MARY *hesitates, breathing deeply.*

YOUNG MARY: Yes . . .

MARY (*voice-over*): I couldn't stop myself . . . I had to say yes.

GREVILLE *nods gravely.*

GREVILLE: Right . . .

INT. KITCHEN. LATE AFTERNOON

We cut to MARY *in the kitchen in the present, standing by the window, the winter light on her face.*

MARY: And then he tells me a series of what I can only call horrific things . . . He was very calm . . . very specific – the year, the exact location, and of course all the real names.

FLASHBACK. INT. BASEMENT. NIGHT
We are back in the wine cellar as we glimpse GREVILLE *among the bottles, moving and talking, and the face of* YOUNG MARY *watching him, transfixed.*

MARY (*voice-over*): Names that I have tried very hard to forget ever since. At first I thought I could handle it –
We stay on YOUNG MARY'*s face.*
It's started with something fairly nasty, but not unbearable, about an archbishop who thrashed little boys until they bled and were raw . . . continued even when he was a famous prelate.
We see GREVILLE *talking and moving.*
GREVILLE: He thrashed and thrashed them . . . !
We cut back to MARY *in the kitchen in the present.* JOE *is staring at her.*
MARY: Then he moved on to a famous public figure who'd apparently kept a young woman like a slave in his house . . . degraded her in the most horrible fashion, for year after year . . . There was a story that particularly shocked me, something he himself had directly witnessed about a very senior politician – somebody who had helped lead us through the war – watching a documentary about the Holocaust and coming out of it afterwards and saying to Greville –
We cut back to the past.
GREVILLE: 'The fucking Jews, they were really asking for it!' That's what he said to me, Mary . . .
YOUNG MARY (*very quiet*): That's terrible.
GREVILLE: Yes . . . He seemed very surprised when I went rather quiet after he'd said it.
We see YOUNG MARY'*s face and then we cut to* MARY, *in the present, in the kitchen.*

INT. KITCHEN. LATE AFTERNOON

MARY: There were stories of cruelty to children, there
were stories of the worst kind of prejudice . . . there
were one or two things so disgusting I have never
been able to get them out of my head – I find myself
thinking about them nearly every week, even now . . .
Everything he told me was sordid, and sometimes
unbearably sad, too . . . and I believed every word.
I don't think he was making it up . . . in fact, I know
he wasn't making it up.
We move in on her face.
I mean, I know there are stories you can tell about the
powerful in any age – I'm sure you could collect awful
things now . . . But hearing them pour out, all together,
coming right at me . . .

FLASHBACK. INT. BASEMENT. NIGHT
We cut back to YOUNG MARY *in the wine cellar.*

MARY (*voice-over*): It took me totally by surprise. I liked to
think of myself as very sophisticated and unshockable,
but he really shocked me.
There is silence in the wine cellar.
GREVILLE *lights a cigarette, then looks across at* YOUNG
MARY.
GREVILLE: Nice life I lead?!
YOUNG MARY *is totally silent.*
GREVILLE: There is a line of cruelty, Mary, that I've
watched personally running from before the war right
through to where we are now. (*He smokes for a moment.*)
I think I'm a great witness . . . the many things I've
seen . . . It's just I can never tell people.
YOUNG MARY: Why are you telling me?

GREVILLE: I don't know . . . I really don't know the answer
to that, Mary. (*He smokes.*) Maybe because you seemed
a good person to tell. (*He smokes, his tone more gentle.*)
'The Voice of Youth.'

MARY (*voice-over*): For just a moment I almost felt sorry
for him, he seemed so weighed down with all these
repellent things he knew about, so bursting to share
them with somebody at last . . . But then he said –

GREVILLE: And also perhaps I wanted to tell you because
I wanted to show you something –

YOUNG MARY: Show me what?

GREVILLE: Show you that even though I know all these
things – in one or two instances have actually been in
the house when they happened – I still believe the
alternative is worse.

YOUNG MARY: What's the alternative?

GREVILLE: Reducing everybody and everything to the
same level. (*He smiles.*) Letting the great unwashed
run everything . . .

MARY (*voice-over*): And then suddenly he is all bright and
argumentative –

GREVILLE: Do you agree with me, Mary?

MARY (*voice-over*): – as if after telling me all these disgusting
things, none of it mattered, it's as if what he really
wanted was a little dinner-party political ding-dong . . .
to take me on . . .

GREVILLE (*more steely*): What's your view, Mary?

YOUNG MARY *meets his gaze and then turns away.*

GREVILLE: You are going to run away now, aren't you?

YOUNG MARY: Well, I think I better leave, don't you?

GREVILLE: No, I don't think you should leave.

YOUNG MARY: Well I am going to.

She moves back out into the passage.

GREVILLE: We haven't chosen our bottle yet . . .

YOUNG MARY *is moving away from him. She suddenly*
stops and calls back to him down the length of the passage.
YOUNG MARY: Of course everything you've told me . . .
GREVILLE: Yes?
YOUNG MARY: Will remain completely confidential.
GREVILLE: Naturally . . .
YOUNG MARY: I won't breathe a word.
GREVILLE: Do I really believe that?
YOUNG MARY: Yes – you do believe that.
GREVILLE: If that's what you promise, Mary.
YOUNG MARY: That's what I promise.

A receding shot of GREVILLE *standing in the passage of*
the wine cellar. We track away from him until he is a very
small figure disappearing into darkness.

Suddenly the image bursts into bright white electric
light. The same passage lit by a line of fluorescent lights.

INT. WINE CELLAR. LATE AFTERNOON
The camera is staring at the passage in the brilliant white light.
  JOE *and* MARY *in the present are standing in the passage*
YOUNG MARY *left* GREVILLE *in.*

MARY: It still looks creepy, even with all this light on . . .
    (*She moves a few paces.*) I suppose most basements are
    creepy . . .
JOE: I've never seen a rat down here – so it must be quite
    clean. (*He rattles his big bunch of keys.*) I s'pose so little
    goes on in this house now, there's not much for them
    to eat . . .
    MARY *stops by the wine cellar, all the bottles glistening.*
MARY: And all the wine is still here! Nobody drinks it?
JOE: No.
    MARY *suddenly looks at* JOE.

MARY: You're thinking I shouldn't ever have come down
    here with him, Joe?

JOE: I wasn't thinking that.

MARY: That when he asked me that question, a question
    that changed the course of my life – 'Do you want to
    hear the real story?' – I should have said no. (*She
    smiles at* JOE.) Would you have said no?

JOE: I don't think so . . .

    MARY *stares back down the passage. We hear the sound of
    footsteps running and running, echoing loudly all along
    the basement. And then we begin to hear, faintly at first,
    the sound of an operatic aria.*

    We cut back to the past and see YOUNG MARY *running
    along the labyrinth of passages.*

MARY (*voice-over*): As I ran away, I could hear the singing
    in the distance and it is getting louder and louder . . .
    which meant I was going in the right direction – never
    has opera sounded so good! When he could no longer
    see me – I ran for my life.

INT. RECEPTION ROOM. NIGHT

We see YOUNG MARY, *looking startled and harassed, emerging
into the passage outside the glowing reception room and then
entering the room fast, so she can be among people.*

    *She sits near the back of the room and tries to calm down.
There are only about eight other people in the room, drinking
brandy as the young women sing to them.*

MARY (*voice-over*): I told myself as I sat there I would let
    everything go, let it wash away, that by the time I got
    home it would be gone. Of course, within minutes
    of me sitting there I realised that wasn't going to
    happen.

The faces of the young women singing the soothing lovely
aria, we move in on their faces, and then on to the YOUNG
MARY.

MARY (*voice-over*): Because as soon as I was alone with
my thoughts . . . everything he told me became even
more vivid. I knew it would be a struggle to get those
images out of my head. For some reason I started
seeing . . .

We move very close on YOUNG MARY's *eyes, and then*
suddenly we see Pathé newsreels of the late 1950s: the
opening of Parliament, a movie premiere, the crowd
gathering for Ascot in their ridiculous hats, debs queuing
outside Buckingham Palace in readiness to make their
curtsies before the Queen.

MARY (*voice-over*): . . . this newsreel footage . . . and I was
thinking all these things he's told me are running
underneath – underneath these events . . .

We cut back to YOUNG MARY's *face.*

MARY (*voice-over*): And then something else dawned on
me. Because he had been so specific, every date, every
name, people that were still alive – he had told me
everything. When he came back into the room –

We see GREVILLE *entering with* LIZA *by his side. He*
stands bantering with a very elderly man at the front of
the room and LIZA *beams down at the man too.*

MARY (*voice-over*): – he was carrying on as if nothing had
just happened, only occasionally glancing in my
direction . . . But I realised . . . he has told me all
these things which he might not have told anybody
else – so he is not going to let go of me that easily.
Just running away from him in the cellar isn't going
to finish the business.

We see GREVILLE *chatting to* LIZA *and filling up her glass*
with more wine.

MARY (*voice-over*): I knew I had to be very careful if he
    wasn't to think he had some hold over me. As I
    watched him . . . I thought it best to seem like I was
    making light of the whole matter, like he had done
    down in the cellar – that what had happened was of
    no significance. So I smiled at him . . .
    We see YOUNG MARY *lighting a cigarette, blowing smoke,*
    smiling across at GREVILLE.
MARY (*voice-over*): I even gave him a little wave, like, that's
    all over, those secrets you told me are gone, flushed
    away . . .

INT. CELLAR. LATE AFTERNOON
We cut back to the present. MARY *is shivering slightly in the*
subterranean passage.

MARY: Let's get out of here, Joe. (*She turns.*) Come on . . .

*She launches off down the passage then stops. She turns
to* JOE.

MARY (*slight laugh*): I need you to lead me, Joe. I don't
know how to get out of this bloody place!

JOE *beckons with his large bunch of keys.*

JOE: It's this way.

INT. STAIRWELL. LATE AFTERNOON

JOE *and* MARY *emerge from the basement into the stairwell
on the ground floor. Above them is the decorative eighteenth-
century ceiling and skylight. It is the last moments of daylight.
A winter evening closing in.*

MARY: That's better . . . Thank you, Joe.

She moves into the shadow for a moment as JOE *locks the
door to the basement. As he turns back, he is just in time
to see her taking a surreptitious swig from a little flask in
her coat pocket.* MARY *realises he has seen this.*

MARY: Just keeping out the winter cold . . .

JOE: Did you get away from him? Away from this man?

MARY: That was my intention, Joe. And for that to be
possible, I knew I needed to see him again . . .

She glances up at the stairwell and then back at JOE.

MARY: I would be so vague when I saw him, so forgetful –
he'll realise he had no hold over me. I knew he could
still do me real professional harm if he chose . . .

FLASHBACK. INT. STAIRWELL/FIRST FLOOR. NIGHT

*The camera glances up at the stairwell again. Now it is night in
the past. The staircase is lit by candles; there are clusters of them
all the way up the stairs, floating on water in large dishes. The
whole house is twinkling and flickering romantically.*

MARY (*voice-over*): It was the first time I had been invited
to spend the night here. Mr Graham had planned a
weekend of events – we had been to the tennis at
Wimbledon, in the morning we were going on his
launch down the river. As always there was a small
group of guests and they were all very famous. (*She
laughs.*) And then there was me . . . ! But no Greville
White.

*The camera is moving along the first-floor passage which
is also lit by candles. We hear the faraway sound of
women's voices singing Edwardian ballads.*

Mr Graham's theme for the evening seemed to be
Edwardian music hall . . . The house was ringing with
these old songs from before the First World War. It
was very nostalgic.

We cut back to MARY *staring up the empty staircase in the
present.*

INT. RECEPTION ROOM. NIGHT

*We cut back to the past. We are in the main reception room,
which is also lit with candelabra full of candles.*

*The three young women are singing a medley of Edwardian
songs, accompanied by another young woman on the piano.*

*The women are dressed in exceptionally revealing low-cut
evening dresses, almost spilling out of them. They move in a
very suggestive way as they sing the songs.*

YOUNG MARY *is standing in the corner of the room in an
exquisite yellow dress watching the singers.*

MR GRAHAM *and a group of men in dinner jackets are
sitting at the back of the room smoking cigars and watching the
women sing.* YOUNG MARY *in her yellow dress stands out
among all these men.*

MARY (*voice-over*): His favourite singers were performing
these songs for him. For some reason they were
wearing practically nothing – his own private cabaret,
I suppose . . . ! I had a feeling it might turn into some
sort of striptease . . . one of the reasons I escaped
upstairs.

*We stay for a moment on the young women as they sing
for* MR GRAHAM. *At the end of the song all the men
applaud and continue to stare at the women. As we watch
this we hear* MARY's *voice-over.*

MARY (*voice-over*): I remember I was feeling really excited.
I had just been given a really important assignment
at work, to do a series of articles in America. It was
going to be my first visit there . . . I was feeling really
good about things . . .

YOUNG MARY (*approaching* MR GRAHAM): Mr Graham,
I had a fantastic day, thank you. I'm heading to
America soon, I'm doing a few articles out there.

MR GRAHAM: How wonderful.

YOUNG MARY: Yes, it's a fantastic opportunity. Although
I am only going for a really short time, I'm really
excited. Goodnight.

MARY (*voice-over*): I decided to go to bed early . . . It was a
lovely summer night, really warm . . .

We follow YOUNG MARY *climbing the staircase, her yellow
dress billowing out, surrounded by hundreds of candles,
and then we track behind her, towards her guest bedroom.*

INT. BLUE BEDROOM/PASSAGES. NIGHT
We cut to YOUNG MARY *reaching the door of her guest bedroom
and pushing it open. She sees a beautiful room with blue walls.
It is also lit by candles, and there are flowers all round the room.*

We cut back to MARY *in the present, staring up at the passage for a moment from the stairwell. A look of apprehension in her eyes.*

Then we cut back to YOUNG MARY *standing in the middle of her blue bedroom in her yellow dress.*

We then cut to the singers in their provocative dresses, performing for the men in the reception room. The young women start singing, 'How much is that doggie in the window?' as the men's eyes gaze at them.

INT. BLUE BEDROOM. NIGHT
We cut back to YOUNG MARY *sitting on the side of her bed. She is taking her shoes off, about to undress. There is a knock on the door.*

YOUNG MARY: Who is it?

GREVILLE: It's me. Greville.

YOUNG MARY: I'm sorry, I'm just going to bed.

GREVILLE: I don't need to come in, I've just got something here for you.

> YOUNG MARY *opens the door.* GREVILLE *is standing in the doorway with two pudding bowls.*

GREVILLE: I thought you might like some strawberries. I missed the tennis – but I brought the strawberries! (*He grins.*) With clotted cream! Do you want some?

> YOUNG MARY *looks at him with a vague smile.*

YOUNG MARY: Thank you. That's very kind. I'll have a spoonful.

> GREVILLE *stands in the doorway, pointedly not crossing the threshold, eating his strawberries.*

GREVILLE: It's all right, I don't need to come in.

> YOUNG MARY *sits demurely on the side of her bed, with the strawberries.*

GREVILLE: You look really well.

YOUNG MARY: Thank you. I am.

> GREVILLE *stops eating his strawberries. He hesitates. The sound of the women singing drifts up from downstairs.*

GREVILLE: I just wanted to say, Mary . . . about the last time we saw each other . . .

YOUNG MARY (*vague smile*): Oh yes, when you made that big salad.

GREVILLE: Yes, there was the salad. And then there was what I told you.

YOUNG MARY: Oh yes. (*Slight laugh.*) Something about a film star and dogs!

GREVILLE: Yes . . . that was part of it. (*Glancing across at her.*) Amongst other things. I just wanted to explain why –

YOUNG MARY: You don't have to.

GREVILLE (*sharply*): Please. I just wanted to say I really didn't mean to upset you.

YOUNG MARY: Was I upset? I don't think so. (*She smiles reassuringly.*)

GREVILLE: Right. That's good! (*With feeling.*) I'm glad you weren't.

FLASHBACK. INT. RECEPTION ROOM. NIGHT
We cut back to the young women in the reception room. One of them is lying stretched out on the piano, like a nightclub chanteuse, singing an old ballad straight at the four men at the back of the room.

INT. BLUE BEDROOM. NIGHT
We cut back to GREVILLE *eating the last strawberries in his bowl. He chuckles.*

GREVILLE: Sorry – eating these, like this . . . just reminded me of something. (*He glances at* YOUNG MARY.) Since I didn't upset you last time, I'll risk one more . . . one more little image.

YOUNG MARY *tries not to show her alarm.*

YOUNG MARY: Please, it's late –

GREVILLE: No, no, this is tiny, funny – not like the other ones. It was in a private room, at a gentlemen's club, the Beefsteak Club.

INT. WOOD-PANELLED ROOM. NIGHT

A door opens abruptly, the camera discovers a group of five men and GREVILLE *sitting round a dinner table in dinner jackets in a private room at a club. All the men are eating some very sticky Greek pudding.*

GREVILLE (*voice-over*): A group of us were trying out – for reasons I don't remember – a series of ghastly over-sweet Greek puddings, with names like *galaktoboureko*; they were so sticky, it was like eating glue . . .
We see the men feeling their teeth as the pudding sticks in their mouths; it is clinging to their teeth and their tongues.
And as we were trying to unstick ourselves . . .
these men were saying – very senior figures in the government – 'You know how I hate niggers, but we are going to have to give them something, especially in Africa . . . ' and somebody else is saying, 'The niggers will never be able to run anything, it's madness!' I mean, it was very standard stuff, but as they talked they were all fiddling with their teeth, their mouths were literally being gummed up.

INT. BLUE BEDROOM. NIGHT
Sharp cut to YOUNG MARY.

YOUNG MARY: Why are you telling me this?

GREVILLE: I thought you'd like that picture – these men sitting around . . . 'I hate the niggers' – and all this syrup in their mouths . . .

YOUNG MARY: And did you agree with them?

GREVILLE: I didn't say that, did I?

YOUNG MARY *puts down the bowl of strawberries.*

YOUNG MARY: Thank you for the strawberries. I need to go to sleep now.

GREVILLE: Of course . . . I just have one other thing I want to give you.

He is still standing in the doorway, scrupulously not crossing the threshold.

YOUNG MARY: No, no, it's late and –

GREVILLE'*s tone is suddenly really intense, almost pleading.*

GREVILLE: Please, just let me for a moment . . .

He moves in the doorway as if searching for the right words.

I know you think I am a snob, Mary, that I'm only interested in the rich and the titled, and maybe that's true up to a point – but it's not the whole story, Mary . . .

YOUNG MARY: I really don't know what you think or believe – and I don't need to know.

GREVILLE: I like taste, refinement . . . (*Intensely.*) I really value that. I don't think that's a crime. The idea of everything being reduced to total mediocrity, to the lowest common denominator – that does terrify me . . . I hate the common herd.

YOUNG MARY: So you must hate me then, mustn't you?

GREVILLE *stares across at her, at her young face in her yellow dress.*

YOUNG MARY: Because that's where I'm from.

GREVILLE: You really imagine that I'd be here if that was what I felt? Is that what you think of me, Mary? I'd be really disappointed if that is what you thought of me . . .

MARY (*voice-over*): I had my chance then . . .

INT. BLUE BEDROOM. WINTER EVENING

We cut to MARY *standing in the present in the doorway exactly where* GREVILLE *had stood.* JOE *is standing inside the room by the bed. The room has the same blue wallpaper, though it is now lit by just one naked light bulb hanging in the centre of the room.*

MARY: I could tell him what I thought of him now . . . I so wish I could have found the words, Joe. I often think about that moment, imagine it again in my head – and when I do that, I really demolish him, I'm incredibly eloquent . . . But I was a very young woman, sitting on the end of a bed – and there was this older man playing some strange game with me . . . *We are close on* MARY'*s eyes.*
I don't think I did too badly . . .

FLASHBACK. INT. BLUE BEDROOM. NIGHT

YOUNG MARY: You want to know what I think of you, Greville? I think you're a bit sad.

GREVILLE (*very quiet*): Sad? In what way, Mary?

YOUNG MARY: You're very clever of course . . . but for some reason you see me as a threat. A threat to your nice life in country houses. Why on earth you should think that I don't know ... Maybe it's because I'm young, and a woman, of course, and you feel I don't show enough respect or something ...

She stares straight at him from the bed.

And you want to stop me being a threat. I think that's what you're doing ... And that's rather sad, don't you think? Somebody like you spending so much energy over somebody like me ...

She moves up to him with her bowl of strawberries.

Thank you for the strawberries and goodnight.

GREVILLE (*takes the bowl*): Right ...

He puts the two bowls down on a table just inside the room and slips his hand inside his pocket.

If that's what you feel, Mary, you probably won't want this then?

He takes an envelope out of his pocket.

But I really would urge you to take it.

YOUNG MARY: I don't want it, whatever it is.

GREVILLE's *tone becomes really intense again.*

GREVILLE: Please look inside ... and then I'll go. I promise.

YOUNG MARY *takes hold of the door handle so she can close the door. Then, leaning on the door, she reluctantly opens the envelope. Inside she finds a Yale door key on a piece of red ribbon. Attached to the ribbon is a card with an address on it.*

YOUNG MARY: What is this? (*She laughs nervously.*) The key to the wine cellar?

GREVILLE: It's the key to my house.

YOUNG MARY: To your house?!

GREVILLE: Yes ... and it doesn't mean what you think it does.

YOUNG MARY: Whatever it means – I don't want it!

GREVILLE (*his tone quietly intense*): I want you to consider this very carefully, Mary – do you understand? This isn't a trick or some cheap gesture. I want you to have the imagination to accept it – the key to my house. You can come there whenever you want . . . You can visit just once or many times . . . just drop by, let yourself in . . . either alone or with a friend . . .

YOUNG MARY: Why on earth would I want to do that?

GREVILLE: I have a wonderful library . . . there are all sorts of things in that house which I have collected over many years . . . over my whole life! Pictures, antiques . . . even movie posters, things you would appreciate. If I happen to be there when you come by . . . I wouldn't try to touch you, not ever. I would leave you to browse as you wanted . . . to use the house as you felt fit. Just a place to stop by . . . I would never attempt to be your lover.
Silence.

YOUNG MARY: Greville . . . that really is too strange –

GREVILLE: I really would urge you not to refuse straight away – please!

YOUNG MARY *turns the key over in her hand.*

YOUNG MARY: How many of these do you hand out to girls each season?

GREVILLE'*s eyes narrow.*

GREVILLE (*very quiet*): That is unkind, Mary. I had that specially made for you. You won't believe me – but I have never done this before, never even thought of doing it . . . I want you to use it, Mary.
He stares at her in her yellow dress in the blue room. She looks so young and poised, although clearly at the moment she is totally unnerved and trying hard not to show it.
I thought we might help each other . . .
GREVILLE'*s tone is quiet, but* YOUNG MARY *detects the threat behind the remark.*

YOUNG MARY: Help each other? In what way?

GREVILLE: In all sorts of ways.

YOUNG MARY: What does that mean?

GREVILLE: Professionally, of course. That goes without
saying.

He stares straight at YOUNG MARY.

GREVILLE: But in other ways, too. Help each other
understand the world . . .

YOUNG MARY: Goodnight, Greville.

GREVILLE: Don't give it back to me now, Mary, please.
Think about it overnight at least!

YOUNG MARY *moves right up to him.*

YOUNG MARY: I've thought about it.

*She presses the key back into his hand and shuts the door
in his face.*

INT. BLUE BEDROOM. WINTER EVENING
We cut to the present. MARY *is in the doorway of the blue
bedroom.*

MARY: And this room looks exactly the same, Joe. (*Almost
angrily.*) Has none of this house been redecorated?!

JOE *is sitting on the end of the bed, deeply involved in
what she has just told him.*

JOE: He didn't come bursting back in, did he? He didn't
knock the door down and come rushing at you?

MARY: No, Joe . . . He was a bit cleverer than that.

She sits next to JOE *on the bed, staring at the blue walls.
We move in on her face.*

MARY: I can still feel that night . . . how warm it was! How
good I felt in that dress . . . (*She feels in her pocket for
her hip flask.*) But I was bloody nervous after he had
gone . . . with that creepy envelope and his key . . .

We see GREVILLE *move away from the door and slowly
walk down the staircase back to the party.*

We cut to the YOUNG MARY *lying on her bed, still in
her yellow dress, staring out, breathing deeply.*

We cut back to MARY *in the present.*

MARY: As soon as he had left – I began to regret I hadn't
really gone for him. I should have torn into him,
screamed at him, 'You'll have no control over me!',
made him afraid of me, and then I might be rid of
him . . .

FLASHBACK. INT. HALL. EARLY MORNING

*The camera moving along the mosaic floor in the stairwell and
out into the hall in very early morning light.*

MARY (*voice-over*): I thought I'd leave very early, get away
from this house, get on with my life, never come back.

We cut to YOUNG MARY *moving across the hall with her
smart overnight bag. There are no staff around that early.
She reaches the front door. Suddenly a voice calls out her
name.* YOUNG MARY *turns.* LIZA, *the young girl we saw
with* GREVILLE, *is sitting in the corner in the shadows.*

LIZA: Hello, Mary . . . I've got a letter for you.

YOUNG MARY: A letter for me?

LIZA: Yes. From Greville.

YOUNG MARY (*as she moves across the hall to get the letter*):
It's very early.

LIZA: Yes, it is, isn't it? Sometimes I love to get up early.

YOUNG MARY (*reaching* LIZA): I don't think we have been
properly introduced . . . I'm Mary Gilbert.

LIZA: And I'm Liza Henton (*She smiles sweetly.*) There,
now we've done it properly.

LIZA gives her the letter.

YOUNG MARY (*taking the letter*): Thank you.

INT. BLUE BEDROOM. THE PRESENT. NIGHT
We cut back to the present. MARY *is sitting with* JOE *on the bed.*

MARY: I felt really nervous then, Joe, right at that moment. It was 5.45 in the morning and Greville had got this young girl to sit up, maybe all night, to intercept me ...

FLASHBACK. INT. HALL. EARLY MORNING
We cut back to the hall, the camera moving towards YOUNG MARY. *She stands with the letter, being watched by* LIZA.

MARY (*voice-over*): She looked so beautiful ... I couldn't help thinking, does he have sex with this girl? Does he keep several of them in his house? Did it all start with them being given keys?
YOUNG MARY: Thank you.
She moves to put the letter in her bag.

LIZA: He said you should read it now, and I should wait to
see if there was a reply.

YOUNG MARY (*firmly*): I'll read it when I get home.

LIZA *fastens her with a look.*

LIZA: He said if you could open it now.

INT. BLUE BEDROOM. NIGHT

MARY: I suddenly thought – what if it was the key again
and I have accepted it unwittingly? . . . Maybe Liza
would tell him I took the key . . . I felt the envelope in
my bag, to see if there was anything in it.

FLASHBACK. INT. HALL. EARLY MORNING
We cut back to YOUNG MARY'*s fingers feeling in the bag,
getting hold of the envelope, sliding along it, looking for the key.
She realises* LIZA *is watching all this.*

LIZA: Why don't you just open it?

YOUNG MARY *begins to open the letter.*

LIZA: No need to be nervous.

YOUNG MARY: I assure you I am not nervous.

We hear GREVILLE'*s voice-over as* YOUNG MARY *reads
the letter.*

GREVILLE (*voice-over*): My dear Mary. You disappointed
me last night. You should have taken the key. Liza has
handed you this letter, just look at her – does she
appear in any way frightened of me? Why don't you
ask her about me?

YOUNG MARY *and* LIZA'*s eyes meet.*

GREVILLE (*voice-over*): Please come out for dinner with me
tonight. So we can settle our differences and part

friends. It would be a much better way for us to end
things . . .

YOUNG MARY *and* LIZA's *eyes meet again.* LIZA *looks at
her enquiringly.*

YOUNG MARY: Thank you for waiting. There's no reply.

LIZA: No reply at all?

LIZA *stares straight at* YOUNG MARY.

YOUNG MARY: No.

EXT. A PARK. WINTER MORNING

We see a shot of YOUNG MARY *walking up a steep path in a
London park in winter light. The park is almost entirely empty
and looking ghostly in the morning mist.*

*One nanny in her grey uniform is pushing a pram down the
hill in the opposite direction to* YOUNG MARY. *At first the
nanny and the pram are just distant shapes on the horizon.*

We are tracking behind YOUNG MARY *as she walks rapidly,
her shoulders hunched against the cold.*

MARY (*voice-over*): For a few days nothing at all happened.
I thought I'd got rid of him, life was going to go on as
normal. But then my trip to America was cancelled . . .
They said to me – my bosses – they had decided the
timing wasn't 'quite right'.

*The pram is a little nearer, its wheels squeaking as the
hatchet-faced nanny pushes it in the winter light.*

And then a few months later my contract wasn't
renewed. I was told my style of journalism – the voice
of youth – was no longer in fashion!

The nanny in her fifties uniform is level with YOUNG
MARY *now. She glances towards* YOUNG MARY, *who is
hunched and preoccupied as she walks. The nanny gives
her a rather hostile look.* YOUNG MARY *carries on walking*

*to a temple in the park and shelters in it to have a
cigarette.*

MARY (*voice-over*): I wasn't too disturbed – I felt I could
get a job at any national newspaper after the success
I'd had. But one by one, for a whole variety of
reasons, they said no . . .

*A portly man out for his early-morning walk passes her in
the park and gives* YOUNG MARY *a glinting interested
look.*

INT. BLUE BEDROOM. NIGHT. THE PRESENT

MARY: I heard I was meant to be very difficult and
unreliable (*she laughs*) – and greedy! I realised Greville
was behind it, of course – he was friendly with the
newspaper proprietors and knew a lot about their
personal lives, too.

We are close on MARY. *We cut back to the past for a
moment as we see her hunched younger self sheltering in
the temple. We cut back to the present.*

It seems amazing now, doesn't it, that one person can
have such power over a person's career . . . ? I mean
such far reaching power?

JOE: Didn't you find Greville and make him do something?

MARY *smiles at this.*

MARY: No, Joe, I didn't. I didn't feel any rage, strangely . . .
I thought, what the hell! I've saved a little money, I need
a break. I'll go abroad, travel and write another book . . .

We see a close-up of YOUNG MARY *in her blue hat looking
out from the temple.*

MARY *stares at the blue bedroom for a moment, at the
stark electric light.*

And I did travel, Joe . . . (*She takes another swig from
her hip flask.*) I had a few love affairs . . . (*She smiles.*)

One of which was great fun . . . But somehow I wasn't doing much writing.

A shot of YOUNG MARY *sitting on a park bench in front of the temple, huddled from the wind reading a book.*

We close in on MARY's *eyes.*

But what I did find was – I quite often thought about Greville . . . kept on seeing his face. I couldn't stop that happening . . . One day I decided to come home, Joe –

We track back from YOUNG MARY *sitting on the bench in the cold wind. The image dissolves to white and then into a haze of cigarette smoke.*

FLASHBACK. INT. FIRST SIXTIES PARTY. ORANGERY PASSAGE. DAY

MARY (*voice-over*): I came back here. I was going out with a young painter at that time who had become very fashionable, and he was invited by Mr Graham. And my lover said, 'Why don't you come?' and I thought, why not? If Greville happens to be there – which seems highly unlikely after all this time – what can he do to me now? And I thought, maybe I can do something to him, be devastating . . . be witty . . . reduce him to a little heap!

We enter behind YOUNG MARY *and* ZACH *through the door of the downstairs passage, into the orangery of the big house, and track behind them past guests who are lining the passage. Young people dressed in sixties clothes. As they go round the corner,* ZACH *turns to* YOUNG MARY *and touches her affectionately, whispering. We see* YOUNG MARY *for the first time properly in her sixties clothes, dazzling in her short skirt, her eyes sparkling.*

MARY (*voice-over*): Britain had changed, of course, while I had been abroad . . . even Mr Graham had changed!

He had torn out the beautiful conservatory in the house and built this horrible modern room, in an attempt to be 'with it'!

ZACH: You look great.

YOUNG MARY: Good. (*She smiles.*) Coming back here . . . I wanted to!

They begin to climb the spiral staircase.

INT. MAIN SIXTIES ROOM. DAY

We cut to YOUNG MARY *and* ZACH *emerging at the top of the staircase. They stare across the main sixties room crowded with young guests. They begin to move around the edge of the room towards us,* ZACH *greeting people he knows. They look a handsome couple,* ZACH *proud to be showing off this older woman, who is glamorous and experienced.*

ZACH *and* YOUNG MARY *in conversation with three other young people.* ZACH *puts his arm round* YOUNG MARY.

ZACH: She used to write some really racy stuff. Didn't you?

YOUNG MARY (*smiles*): What do you mean used to . . . ?!

ZACH: And some quite heavy stuff too. (*He grins.*) She can really write, this one!

YOUNG MARY (*laughs*): That's good to know! (*She touches him.*) Must put that on the back of the next book – a quote from you – 'I think she can write'!

Then ZACH *is distracted by another guest and the couple they were talking to question* YOUNG MARY *about her writing.*

YOUNG MARY: Where have I been ? I've been abroad . . . in the sun, working of course, yes, writing and planning. (*She leans forward to hear what they are asking her.*) What am I planning? . . . I'm planning a trilogy of

novels about now . . . Yes, it is rather ambitious, yes . . .
Has it got a title? . . . Yes, I think so . . . I think the
title will definitely have the word 'change' in it . . .
something about change . . .

We see YOUNG MARY *suddenly notice* GREVILLE *on the
other side of the room. We cut back to the present.*

MARY (*voice-over*): And there he was suddenly! Right there.
All trussed up in a waistcoat – though it was summer.
He looked suddenly from another age . . . (*Slight
laugh.*) Like one of his wines! Trying to weave his
spell, as he worked the room.

We cut back to the past. YOUNG MARY *is watching*
GREVILLE *as he holds forth some distance away.*

GREVILLE: It's a bit like this room – you know, fashion, the
love of the new, soon we will be nostalgic for glamour
again, and long dresses, and the funny old conservatory
that used to be here! (*He drinks.*) All these short
skirts, legs walking down the street – you don't see
faces any more coming towards you, just an army of
legs . . . And it's the same with these new movies,
people don't want their noses rubbed along the
kitchen floor, see actors dirty fingernails and with
miners' dust pouring out of their ears – least of all do
they want to see the working class copulating. I always
walk out immediately when they start rutting on the
screen . . . and I am not the only one.

As YOUNG MARY *and* ZACH *stand by the Formica bar,*
ZACH *notices her watching* GREVILLE *intently.*

ZACH: Who is that guy?

YOUNG MARY: Somebody I used to know a long time ago.
We once nearly shared a salad in this very house . . .
(*She watches* GREVILLE *for a moment.*) And we did eat
some strawberries together . . . (*Her is voice quiet, close
to a whisper.*) With clotted cream . . .

INT. SIXTIES ROOM. NIGHT. THE PRESENT
*A sudden cut. A line of modern strip-lighting comes on with a
jolt. We cut to the sixties room in the present at night. It is a
stark and forbidding place. Its decor looks absurdly dated, there
is a bar counter that jabs right out into the room. There are a
couple of curved Formica tables, and there is a large expanse of
empty floor with just two sixties chairs in the corner.*

MARY: Oh God . . . it is an ugly room isn't it?
  JOE *is pacing up and down in the middle of the room,
  getting agitated.*
JOE: Didn't you go up to him? At this party? Didn't you
  say something? You should have got hold of him,
  yanked him in front of people! (*He waves his arms.*)
  Did you do that? Did you say, 'You fucking prick,
  you've done this to me! Now you fucking do something
  about it – and get me my job back!'
MARY: I didn't say that, Joe, no.
  JOE *stares at her.*
JOE: You didn't?!
MARY: I couldn't.
JOE (*loud*): Why not?
MARY (*her voice fragile*): Don't get impatient with me, Joe –
  please!
JOE: Sorry . . . didn't mean to shout . . . I want you to get
  this fucker!

FLASHBACK. INT. SIXTIES ROOM. BRIGHT SUNLIGHT
*The camera moving through the party, the faces of the young
guests laughing.*

MARY (*voice-over*): It wasn't going to be easy, Joe . . .
  I realised at once I had made a big mistake going

back . . . For one thing, I felt a bit old-fashioned, everything had moved on while I had been on my travels . . .

We move with the YOUNG MARY *at the party.*

MARY (*voice-over*): I was wearing the right clothes of course . . . but inside I felt a stranger . . .

We cut back to MARY *in the present.*

MARY: It rarely pays to be in the vanguard of things, Joe – to be one of the first; you are superseded very quickly!

We cut back to the sunlit room in the past. We see YOUNG MARY *standing with* ZACH *staring around the party.*

MARY (*voice-over*): But much more important than that – I wasn't there in my own right, I was just with my boyfriend. And suddenly this made me feel very small – I was thinking I used to be invited here when I was a fashionable writer . . .

In amongst them all is GREVILLE, *holding court, pontificating.* YOUNG MARY *avoids his gaze as he glances around the room.*

ZACH (*spies somebody he wants to talk to across the room*): Just want to talk somebody over there . . . about a picture.

YOUNG MARY: Don't be long.

YOUNG MARY *is alone, standing at the Formica bar watching the other guests, their confident faces, their new clothes, the women displaying their bodies, their lack of inhibition.*

GREVILLE: People want fantasy, stories, beautiful worlds to escape into . . . that's always been the case and always will be . . . !

We see YOUNG MARY *moving off and slipping away from* GREVILLE *down the staircase.*

INT. SECOND SIXTIES ROOM. NIGHT
We see YOUNG MARY *entering the second sixties room, the one downstairs where the buffet is laid out. There are huge bowls of Turkish delight and other foods of the moment displayed.*
    YOUNG MARY *moves up to the table and helps herself.*

YOUNG MARY (*to another passer-by*): Can't go wrong with
    Turkish delight! (*She laughs.*) And probably the Turks
    have never heard of it!
    The passer-by looks at her in surprise.
    Sorry, I was just gabbling . . .
    Suddenly she senses something and sees GREVILLE *is
    helping himself at the other end of the buffet. This is the
    nearest they have been to each other.*
        *He looks up and gives her a small polite nod. He then
    moves sideways away from her, to another corner of the
    room, where he begins to talk to a group of young people.*
        Slight time cut. A few moments later. YOUNG MARY *in
    the far corner of the room eating the Turkish delight,
    watching* GREVILLE, *who is holding forth.*
        We see YOUNG MARY *keeping away from* GREVILLE *in
    the corner of the room.*
MARY (*voice-over*): A tiny thing happened at this party . . .
    that had a big effect on me.
GREVILLE: No, no, a lot of what they say is new about
    these movies has in fact been done before loads of
    times and much better . . .
    MR GRAHAM *is standing with* YOUNG MARY *watching*
    GREVILLE *hold court.*
MR GRAHAM: Greville likes to talk, doesn't he?
    YOUNG MARY *smiles, but is trying not to look at*
    GREVILLE.
GREVILLE: The difference is – before it was done with
    style and by people who were true artists; that is

why their work hasn't dated. Unlike this new breed
now, who are addicted to gimmicks and the latest
fad –

MARY (*voice-over*): And this man suddenly piped up – I
think he was a musician –

MUSICIAN: That's complete crap. Everything you've said is
just such utter bollocks!

MR GRAHAM *and* YOUNG MARY *are looking on at this,
shocked by what just happened.*

MARY (*voice-over*): And this young man just put down
his drink and walked straight out of the room . . . No
respect for this older man in a waistcoat – he just gave
it to him and went.

GREVILLE: What a charming young man. Fascinating that
he wanted to share his opinion with us.

YOUNG MARY *is watching this scene and* GREVILLE'*s
glinting little eyes.*

MARY (*voice-over*): I thought, I should have done that! Why
don't I do that to Greville?

The camera is close to GREVILLE *as he moves around the
room looking for somebody else to talk to. And then it is
close to* YOUNG MARY *as she moves on the other side of
the room keeping her distance.*

MARY (*voice-over*): But then I realised I could never talk to
Greville like that – brutal, rude . . .

We see YOUNG MARY *surrounded by the young musicians
and artists.*

MARY (*voice-over*): I don't know – maybe because I belonged
to another time . . . I don't know why I couldn't . . .
Because I was afraid. I couldn't even go up to him at
that party. He is looking for someone else to talk to,
to engage with – and I am almost hiding . . . !

We see GREVILLE'*s sharp eyes scouring the party. He finds*
YOUNG MARY.

MARY (*voice-over*): And suddenly he looks at me, he looks across at me . . . and though he didn't say anything, I could hear him saying –
Their eyes meet.

GREVILLE: But you're still mine . . .
We see him mouthing.
But you're still mine, Mary.
YOUNG MARY *stares at him transfixed. She wants to mouth the words, 'No I'm not . . . I am not.' But though she tries, nothing will come out. She can't form the words.*
GREVILLE *is staring at her, as* YOUNG MARY *wants desperately to get out of the room, but she doesn't want to appear to be fleeing.*

MARY (*voice-over*): I tried not to run, not to look like I was fleeing from his presence . . .
Suddenly some people obscure GREVILLE's *view of* YOUNG MARY *and she has the chance to leave without him seeing her go. We follow her out of the room.*

MARY (*voice-over*): And I didn't want to creep out of there either . . . But I got away from this house as quick as I could.

INT. THE PRESENT. SIXTIES ROOM. NIGHT

JOE: You left here without saying anything to him?
MARY: That's right. I left him looking for me . . .
JOE: But you did speak to him again, didn't you? You didn't just leave it?!
Pause.
MARY: There is not a simple answer to that, Joe . . .
JOE *is staring at her.*
JOE: What do you mean?
We stay on MARY's *face.*
JOE: Go on . . .

MARY *takes another sip from her flask.*
MARY: I'll try to show you, Joe . . .

FLASHBACK. INT. BEDSIT. DAY
We cut to YOUNG MARY *lying on a bed in a bedsit. She is wearing knickers and a T-shirt. She is smoking.*
The room is not very large and the curtains are drawn against the sunlight. There is a sink in the corner, and the whole room is decorated with sixties bric-a-brac. It is cluttered and claustrophobic.
The camera drifts along the bed and up to YOUNG MARY*'s face as she smokes.*

MARY (*voice-over*): For the next few months, maybe a year, I sunk myself into my love affair – with the artist . . .
We see the artist, ZACH, *sitting in the corner of the room, very slowly rolling a joint.*
MARY (*voice-over*): He was getting really successful, almost famous, but he was very careful with money – extremely mean, in fact! So for a time we lived in this bedsit . . . and he disappeared for days on end to his studio . . .
We see ZACH *slowly finishing the joint and lighting it. He is still sitting in the corner of the room, barefoot and with fashionably paint-splattered jeans.*
MARY (*voice-over*): When he wasn't painting – he was thinking deep thoughts . . .

INT. THE PRESENT. SIXTIES ROOM. NIGHT
MARY *smiles.*

MARY: He had an awful lot of deep thoughts it seems . . . none of which I ever got to hear . . .

FLASHBACK. INT. BEDSIT. SUMMER EVENING
The air is thick with smoke. ZACH *is lying on his stomach in the corner of the room, smoking another joint and staring at the wall.* YOUNG MARY *is curled at the end of the bed, in a very short skirt.*

MARY (*voice-over*): The room was full of smoke most of the time – as well as his thoughts. And I started –

We see YOUNG MARY'*s hand reach down and pick up a wine glass, half full of wine. There are two more empty wine glasses in the shadow of the bed.*

MARY (*voice-over*): – having a little tipple . . . at various moments in the day – I found it helped the 'creative flow' . . .

ZACH suddenly stands up and then lets out a yell.

ZACH: Shit! Fuck!

He hobbles around the room rubbing one of his bare feet.

I nearly cut myself . . . fuck! (*He rubs his foot.*)

I stepped on one of your bloody wine glasses . . . !

I TOLD YOU SO MANY TIMES – DON'T LEAVE GLASSES ON THE FLOOR! OK?!

YOUNG MARY *sips her glass.*

ZACH: It's a real pigsty in here! . . . You gotta clear it all up! YOU UNDERSTAND?!

YOUNG MARY: Yeah . . . I understand. (*She looks up from the bed.*) I'll write it down a hundred times . . . (*She sips her glass.*) . . . 'It's a real pigsty in here' . . .

ZACH: And then what are you going to do about it . . . ?

YOUNG MARY: What am I going to do about it?

ZACH: Yes?

YOUNG MARY: Well, maybe I'll start by making a list of all the things of yours I am not allowed to throw out – or even move in some cases . . . (*Mock-horrified.*) 'What have you done Mary, you've moved the cornflake packet . . . ?!'

ZACH: That's complete shit.

YOUNG MARY: What's complete shit?

ZACH: I have never ever said to you, 'You've moved the cornflakes.' That's a total lie –

YOUNG MARY: Oh, I'm lying now, am I?!

ZACH: When have I said that to you? Come on?!

YOUNG MARY: You're always saying things like that – just the other day you accused me of throwing out that

stupid little green cloth that you're forever wiping the
gramophone with . . .

ZACH (*coldly, staring down at her*): Just clean the place up –
OK? (*Pause.*) After all, you've got the time, haven't
you?

YOUNG MARY: Unlike you, you mean?!

ZACH: Yes.

Pause. He stares down at her.

I don't know what you do all day, Mary . . . I really
don't.

Time cut. We see YOUNG MARY *in a different dress sitting
at her desk. It is almost dusk outside. She has her back to
us and is writing on a large pad of paper. The camera is
moving slowly towards her across the room.*

MARY (*voice-over*): I was beginning to write again . . .
another attempt at a novel. Outside the window all
sorts of new things were happening . . . I felt I should
be able to catch those . . . describe them.

*The camera pauses for a moment. It is still some distance
from her as she sits beneath the window.*

But the funny thing was . . .

We cut to MARY *in the present.*

MARY: But the funny thing was . . .

We cut back to the bedsit in the past.

MARY (*voice-over*): It didn't matter whether I started the
story on a train . . . or in the desert . . . or outside
Buckingham Palace, or with people waterskiing in the
South of France . . . wherever I started the story –

The camera is curling up to YOUNG MARY, *almost
reaching her now. We cut back to* MARY *in the present.*

MARY: Always . . .

We cut back to the camera reaching YOUNG MARY *in the
past. Peering over her shoulder. We cut to* MARY *in the
present.*

It always led back to the cellar and Greville.

FLASHBACK
We see GREVILLE *turning towards* YOUNG MARY *in the cellar.*
We then see him staring directly at the camera.

INT. BEDSIT. MIDDAY LIGHT
We cut back to YOUNG MARY. *She is wearing a vest and*
shorts. She is sitting at her desk typing vigorously on a portable
yellow typewriter.

MARY (*voice-over*): One day I changed to writing directly
    on a typewriter . . . Up to then I had always done the
    first draft in longhand. It was a nice day. There were
    church bells outside the window . . . somebody was
    getting married down the street.
    We hear the outpouring of wedding bells.
    And I was flying, absolutely flying with my story . . .
    We see her typing faster and faster, as the bells ring out.
    We move from her face to her typing fingers and then back
    to her face. And the sound begins to subtly change, the
    typewriter begins to dominate the bells, until we can no
    longer hear the bells.
      And then the typing becomes the sound of a ping-pong
    ball smashing against the mosaic floor of the hall.

FLASHBACK
We see the image of GREVILLE *thrashing the ping-pong ball in*
the hall. We see YOUNG MARY'*s face.*

INT. SIXTIES ROOM. NIGHT

MARY: And then I wasn't flying any more . . .

We stay on her for a moment.

Each time this happened my confidence took a further little knock . . . When you have success . . . without really thinking about it when you are very young . . . when you are not quite sure how you did all that, your confidence can go amazingly quickly when things go wrong. (*She smiles.*) Escape was not proving easy, Joe . . .

INT. BEDSIT. EVENING

We cut back to the bedsit. A high shot. YOUNG MARY *is lying in the middle of the floor staring upwards at the ceiling. There is a small mirror propped up against the wall. She turns her head and stares at herself in the mirror. We move in on her face in the mirror.*

MARY (*voice-over*): I knew a lot of people, friends, acquaintances, who had become successful around that time and then destroyed themselves with drink and drugs.

We cut back to the high shot. A little closer to YOUNG MARY *this time.*

MARY (*voice-over*): I decided – I was definitely not going to be one of them! Try my hardest . . .

INT. THE PRESENT. SIXTIES ROOM. NIGHT

JOE (*smiles*): Good.

MARY: I pulled myself together.

JOE: Great!

FLASHBACK. INT. STAIRCASE. LARGE HOUSE. NIGHT
We cut to the grand staircase of a large house we have not seen before. There is the sound of loud rock music. Draped along the staircase, and staring down from one of the upper landings are several young women in short sixties skirts and a couple of tall young men with floppy hair.

MARY (*voice-over*): I started going out again . . . attending private views with my boyfriend. Of course I knew there was a faint chance I might run into Greville – but I was ready for it . . .

INT. THE PRESENT. SIXTIES ROOM. NIGHT
We cut back to JOE.

JOE: Yeah . . . because you haven't spoken to him about him getting you fired!
MARY: I hadn't, no . . .
JOE: You've gotta speak to him about that . . .
　　　MARY *smiles.*
MARY: That's right . . . and so at one particular private view . . . being held at a house in the country –

FLASHBACK. EXT. LARGE HOUSE IN THE COUNTRY. NIGHT
We cut to the exterior of a medium-sized stately home in the country at night. Light and music are spilling out of the house, and there are lines of white lights draped in the trees outside.

People in fashionable sixties clothes are milling around outside the house and getting into their cars, leaving as the event finishes.

YOUNG MARY *is sitting with her boyfriend on the stone steps that lead up to the entrance of the house.*

MARY (*voice-over*): I was sitting there with my boyfriend, having this awful conversation – we'd been breaking up for months but we were doing it in slow motion . . . a little bit each week.

YOUNG MARY *with a glass in her hand.*

MARY (*voice-over*): But this particular night, what we were saying to each other was fairly terminal.

ZACH: Maybe it's because I need more space. I think I really do need a lot more space.

INT. THE PRESENT. SIXTIES ROOM. NIGHT

MARY (*smiles*): He was too mean to buy more space – so he had to kick me out instead! Naturally I wasn't slow in pointing this out . . .

FLASHBACK. EXT. THE COUNTRY HOUSE. NIGHT
We cut back to YOUNG MARY *and* ZACH *on the steps.*

YOUNG MARY: You know, Zach, the other day I was trying to think of the last thing you bought me, any kind of present . . . it took me several hours. You know what it was? It was a single pink balloon, to celebrate my birthday.

ZACH: I don't believe in birthdays. Never have.

YOUNG MARY: Why doesn't that surprise me?

ZACH: But I know what you'd like . . .

YOUNG MARY: What would I like?

ZACH: You'd like a crate of vodka delivered at the beginning of every week. You'd wake up – there it would be at the end of the bed.

YOUNG MARY (*sharp smile*): Once a week! That certainly wouldn't be enough!

oung Mary contemplates her future.

Mary has tea on her return to the house.

Joe keeps an eye on Mary having let her into the house.

Young Mary at one of Mr Graham's soirées sitting among the living legends.

Greville eats the Greek pudding at the Beefsteak club.

Mary reliving her relationship with Greville.

Young Mary after she has turned down Greville's offer.

Greville and Young Mary in the wine cellar.

Young Mary returns the key to Greville.

Young Mary in the 1960s conservatory on her return to the house.

Young Mary is haunted by Greville as she tries to write.

Greville staring back at Young Mary. 'Help me.'

Greville appears in the park in the present day.

Mary is haunted by Greville as she sits in the park.

ZACH *watches* YOUNG MARY *drink.*

ZACH: You gotta be careful . . .

YOUNG MARY: Careful of what? Of liking this too much, you mean? . . . I do like it, I admit. (*She takes a swig from the glass.*) Well, there have to be some compensations during the day . . . since our life together has been so scintillating recently!
She sips from the glass again.

> *The camera watches the departing guests.*

MARY (*voice-over*): So we were right in the middle of our break-up . . . and there –
We see a familiar figure standing in the drive, talking to some guests.

There was Greville.
We watch GREVILLE *standing among the young guests with the air of somebody who is used to being listened to.*

GREVILLE (*to fashionable-looking young artist and his girlfriend*): I saw you at the Glyn-Parrys' in August . . . don't you remember? No, I think we were sitting quite near each other at dinner . . .

MARY (*voice-over*): He was dressed in his usual old-fashioned way – almost defiantly out of keeping with the times . . . He keeps avoiding catching my eye. He knows I am there . . . I know he has seen me! But he won't look at me . . . He is smiling and trying to gossip with people . . .
We see a shot of LIZA *in a long gold dress. She too is trying to engage people in conversation.*

LIZA (*to artist*): I did enjoy the exhibition. Tell me, were they meant to be people or fruit?

ARTIST: What?

LIZA: The shapes – they looked like fruit to me . . . but somebody said they were meant to be people. (*She laughs merrily.*)

MARY (*voice-over*): And Liza was there as well, and she was dressed very oddly, too . . . almost like her mother might have been.

LIZA (*to a smart-looking man*): I'm having a party in my little flat in Kensington in a few weeks . . . I do hope you'll come. I've tried to get all the most interesting people in London together – but I'm told in fact there are only twelve!

MARY (*voice-over*): She was still very young . . . and yet she looked so out of place.

LIZA (*laughing sweetly*): Apparently there are only twelve interesting people in London – and so it will have to be a very tiny gathering as you can see . . . but you are one of them.

GREVILLE (*to distinguished-looking man*): I don't know if you got my letter? . . . No, the post is terrible, isn't it? No, I've had an idea for a book – I was wondering if we could talk about it . . . No, it's a memoir really, a book of memories and anecdotes. Some of the big events I have witnessed. I think it could make a very lively read . . . you know, my time working with Lloyd George and Churchill – oh yes, I worked on Churchill's papers! I got to know him quite well – I got drunk with him, actually, more than once. One of the few times I have ever successfully managed to get drunk! (*He smiles.*)

MARY (*voice-over*): And nobody seemed that interested in them – it was like their joke on the world, this strange couple weaving some sort of spell, wasn't really working any more . . .

GREVILLE: You will be surprised in more ways than one . . . (*He hands the man his card.*) Give me a ring.
Later we see the distinguished-looking man throwing away GREVILLE*'s card as he gets into his car.*

MARY (*voice-over*): But it was like he knew his power was on the wane . . . The great newspaper proprietors he was close to were now dead or had sold up . . . there was a new government. He didn't have nearly so many influential friends.
We see GREVILLE *lit by the headlights of the departing cars.*

MARY (*voice-over*): He was standing very straight – like he was determined not to be engulfed by this new world . . . a world he had first sensed, maybe, when he had met me –

INT. THE PRESENT. SIXTIES ROOM. NIGHT
We cut back to MARY. *We stay on her face as she thinks about this for a moment.*

MARY (*voice-over*): I was almost relishing watching him like that . . . and I was thinking about Liza.

FLASHBACK. EXT. THE COUNTRY HOUSE. NIGHT
We cut back to YOUNG MARY *watching the scene in front of her,* GREVILLE *in the drive as he waits for his car,* LIZA *standing beside him.*

MARY (*voice-over*): Was that what he had wanted me to become . . . ?
We see GREVILLE *and* LIZA *talking to each other. Then we see a Bentley drive up and* GREVILLE *opening the door for* LIZA.

MARY (*voice-over*): And they both get in. And I am feeling almost relaxed now . . . they are going and nothing has happened . . . Nothing bad has occurred at all . . .

We see the car begin to drive off into the night.
I remember so clearly watching them together in the
back of the car . . . And the car is going . . .

INT. THE PRESENT. SIXTIES ROOM. NIGHT
Close-up of MARY. *And then of* JOE.

MARY (*her voice very quiet*): And then he turns . . . And
stares straight at me . . .

FLASHBACK. EXT. THE COUNTRY HOUSE. NIGHT
*We see the car beginning to pull away down the long drive of
the house.* GREVILLE *turns and stares back through the rear
window.*

MARY (*voice-over*): And he mouths – I can see it so clearly –
he mouths – 'Help me . . . !'
We see GREVILLE's *face. And then see* YOUNG MARY
*watching from the steps transfixed. And then we cut back
to* GREVILLE's *face. And he mouths again: 'Help me,
Mary. Help me!' The car is getting further and further
away, but* YOUNG MARY *can still see* GREVILLE's *face
staring out the back window mouthing: 'Help me, Mary.
Help me!'*

INT. SIXTIES ROOM. NIGHT
And then we see MARY *repeat the line almost under her breath
in the present.*

MARY: 'Help me, Mary . . . ' It wasn't a pathetic cry, Joe . . .
it was quite the reverse. (*She shivers.*) It was terrifying.

FLASHBACK. EXT. DRIVE OF THE COUNTRY HOUSE. NIGHT
We see the car disappearing. GREVILLE's *face getting smaller and smaller.*

INT. THE PRESENT. STAIRWELL. DAY
We cut to MARY *at the bottom of the sixties stairs in the converted conservatory.* JOE *is coming after her down the spiral staircase. He catches up with her.*

MARY: And then I never saw him again, Joe.

> JOE *stares at her startled.*

JOE: What? You didn't? You never, ever said anything about what he had done to you?

MARY: No.

JOE: You didn't ring him up or anything – and say, 'Why should I help you, you did this terrible thing to me?'

MARY: No.

JOE: You didn't write about him in the newspapers?

MARY: No.

> MARY *moves ahead into the downstairs sixties room, the bottom half of the converted conservatory. It is now a faceless empty conference room with hideous curtains.*
>
> *She takes a swig from her flask.* JOE *follows her into the soulless empty room.* MARY *turns towards him. She breathes deeply.*

MARY: I didn't see him again, Joe . . .

> *She pauses.* JOE *is standing in the doorway.*

MARY: Until today . . .

JOE: Today?!

MARY: I saw him today.

JOE: But . . .

> *Their eyes meet.*

He must be really old, mustn't he? I mean, it is a long time ago. He must be an incredibly old man.

There is a pause.

MARY: You would have thought so, wouldn't you, Joe . . .

    JOE *looks at* MARY, *not understanding.*

JOE: What? . . . What do you mean?

    We move in on MARY's *face.*

JOE: Where did you see him?

EXT. LONDON PARK. DAY

We cut to MARY *in the present, walking up the same hill in the London park we saw the* YOUNG MARY *climbing. The same misty winter light. There are very few people around; it is early morning on a cold day. We track behind* MARY.

MARY (*voice-over*): I often go for a walk in the park in the morning . . . and usually it's all right. Alone with one's thoughts, trying not to go over one's life too much, living in the present, planning the next day . . .

    We see her reach the middle of the hill where the nanny had passed her younger self. Now a young female jogger comes out of this mist and runs past her.

So this morning, it was just as normal, I was feeling quite good, really . . .

INT. SIXTIES ROOM. THE PRESENT. NIGHT

We cut back to MARY. *She is staring ahead for a moment,* JOE *watching her.*

MARY: And then –

EXT. THE PARK. DAY.

MARY (*voice-over*): Somebody calls my name . . .

We see her turn. A figure down the hill is calling to her. He is in a dark suit and holding an unfurled umbrella. It is hard to see his face from this distance. A dapper figure at the bottom of the hill, calling.

I couldn't really see him clearly . . . he was a long way away. I stood for a moment.

We see her halfway up the hill staring down at the figure at the bottom. The figure remains still.

I didn't hear my name again . . . so I got on with my walk.

We see her moving along another path in the park.

I'm dimly aware of this figure, a little further on, keeping pace with me, walking along another path . . .

We see the figure in the distance, through the trees, walking along a parallel path.

But he didn't seem to be looking at me . . . I realised he must have been calling somebody else.

We watch the figure disappear among the trees.

So I get to my usual spot – there is a nice little alcove with a bench, I often sit there, for a few minutes . . .

We see MARY *sitting on the bench, in the same temple we saw* YOUNG MARY *sit in. We see a boy snake past on Rollerblades and disappear in the grey light. There is nobody else around. Just the wintry views across the park, the distant rumble of traffic and the sound of the wind. She takes out her hip flask and has a little drink.*

A voice calls: 'Mary.' She looks up. She can see the dapper figure a little better this time. He is about fifty yards away.

I thought, that looks terribly like Greville . . . but of course that's impossible – because this man is not old . . . not old in the least. And Greville was much older than me – and there he is, looking like that, it must be somebody else . . .

INT. SIXTIES ROOM. NIGHT
We cut back to MARY *in the sixties room with* JOE.

MARY: Now I know what you're thinking, it was the drink.
  (*She turns the flask over in her hand.*) This drink in
  fact! And of course you could be right, Joe – because
  this isn't a ghost story.
  We are on her eyes.
  No, this is worse then a ghost story. (*Quiet.*) For me,
  anyway . . .
  JOE *doesn't know what she means.*

JOE: Why?

  MARY *doesn't reply.*

JOE: What happened? Did he come any closer?

  MARY *looks straight at him. Her tone surprisingly forceful
  suddenly.*

MARY: It is very important, because of what happens next,
  for you to realise I don't sit in the park in the morning
  feeling sorry for myself, I hate the idea! I haven't
  spent all these years in self-pity. Do you follow that,
  Joe?

JOE: Yes.

MARY: I had rebuilt a sort of career for myself after the
  setbacks caused by Greville. I've written for magazines
  about gardens, and lifestyle and antiques. I've been
  able to earn a reasonable living . . . Many people
  would think I've been lucky to lead such a life. You
  understand me, Joe?

JOE (*quiet*): Yeah . . . I do.

EXT. PARK. DAY
The camera moves around MARY *on the bench in the park.*
  *We cut sharply to the figure standing on the path in the park,
much nearer than before. He is about twenty yards from* MARY.

He shifts a couple of paces so he moves more into the light. He looks crisp, his shoes shiny, his suit immaculate.

GREVILLE: I thought it was you, Mary.
>   MARY *stares at the figure through the winter light.*
GREVILLE: What are you doing here? All on your own?
>   *He leans on his umbrella. He looks just the same.*
>   I always thought if I saw you again it would be in this park . . . and you would be on your own . . .
MARY (*voice-over*): I couldn't speak, but he seemed to sense what I was thinking . . .
GREVILLE: I'm not alone, in fact . . .
>   MARY *stares behind him, into the trees. There is the wind blowing, rustling, but she sees nobody. Then she glances over to her left, where she sees a bench surrounded by dark bushes where two women in their early sixties are sitting together. She stares at them.*
MARY (*voice-over*): I peered at them . . . they were too far away to see clearly . . . Could one of them have been Liza?
GREVILLE: How's it been, Mary? Everything you hoped?

INT. SIXTIES ROOM. NIGHT
We cut to MARY *with* JOE *in the sixties room.*

MARY: If it was a hallucination, it was a very sustained one. Suddenly he was close . . .

EXT. PARK. DAY
We cut back to the park. There is a shaft of winter sunlight.
GREVILLE *is nearer, his face obscured by a bush near the bench. But he is only about ten feet away.*

GREVILLE: Silly girl, I kept looking for your name . . . I couldn't ever find it.

The camera is very close to MARY. *Her eyes look down. She's unable to meet his gaze. Instead she stares at the ground. She watches his shadow on the path. She fixes her eyes on that rather than look at him.*

GREVILLE: I've had some painful things happen to me, too – we could have helped each other – like I said . . . All you could think was, I wanted to catch you, control you . . .

The sound of the wind. MARY *turns right away, hiding her face, curled away in the alcove.*

GREVILLE: Where've you been all this time, Mary? Where is the bright young girl? (*Softly.*) I can see no sign of her . . . no sign at all.

The boy on his Rollerblades shoots back along the path. MARY *watches him for a second disappear. When she looks back she is alone.* MARY *sits very still. She scours the park, the empty paths, the clumps of winter trees.*

MARY (*voice-over*): The very first thing I thought after he was gone – it was funny – I suddenly understood why he was always there, at Mr Graham's parties! I'd often wondered about that, why he was invited. I realised right then it must have been because he knew something about Mr Graham's past . . . It was such an obvious thought, I don't know why I'd never had it before!

We see an image of the young MR GRAHAM *talking to a group of Nazi storm troopers in the sunlight under some trees in a park in Berlin.*

MARY (*voice-over*): For a moment, I was quite excited, to have worked that out . . .

INT. SIXTIES ROOM. NIGHT
We cut back to MARY *in the sixties room. Her tone changes, quiet, intense.*

MARY: And then suddenly . . . this really strong feeling
    began, that something was shutting, like a door being
    pressed on my face . . . pushing me down, but at the
    same time I kept getting –

EXT. THE PARK. DAY
We see MARY *sitting alone on the park bench.*

MARY (*voice-over*): I kept getting these pictures from the
    past. I promise you, Joe, I don't usually do this. I
    never look back like this . . .
    We see the YOUNG MARY *moving in her yellow dress
    along the passage full of candles.*
MARY (*voice-over*): I started thinking the worst possible
    thoughts – what might have been . . .
    *We see the women singing, we distantly hear the opera. We
    see the older women in their long evening dresses. We see
    the older couples in the hallway of the house, leaving. The
    splendid fur coats going on the women. They move across
    the hall, throwing long shadows.*
    We cut to MARY'*s face in the park and then back to the
    images.*
    How stupid I was to think I could enter that house –
    this house – and to take on that world when I was so
    very young . . . If only I'd been ten years older – or
    been born a few years later, when things were
    different . . .
    *The camera is moving along the candlelit passages. It then
    travels along the subterranean basement towards the cellars
    as the singing rings down, half heard.*

A young woman in that house – it shouldn't ever have happened. And I've never been able to shake it off – all this time. How idiotic is that?!

We turn a corner in the subterranean passage and see GREVILLE *in the distance.*

INT. SIXTIES ROOM. NIGHT

MARY: And I was thinking, too . . . have I used what happened with Greville as an excuse – my whole life – for the loss of my talent . . . ?

She is trying hard not to get emotional in front of JOE.

MARY: And then . . .

EXT. PARK. DAY

We cut back to MARY *on the park bench.*

MARY (*voice-over*): There was this terrible feeling, Joe, right through me. I suppose I have to call it desolation . . . of being so alone.

We are on MARY *in the park.*

I remembered his party trick, of seeing yourself as others see you . . .

We cut wide and see MARY *looking like an old drunk on the park bench. Messy, not at all elegant, in a world of her own, murmuring to herself.*

I suddenly saw myself like that. And all the time, there was this sensation, like the lights being turned down – things are closing in . . . shutting down . . . Suddenly it was difficult to breathe . . .

We see YOUNG MARY *moving confidently into the reception room, her eyes full of humour. We see* GREVILLE

*down in the cellar, raising his arm and miming thrashing
as he tells the story about the archbishop. We see the men
in the Beefsteak Club in their dinner jackets sitting round
the table, with the syrup in their mouths. And then we
move in on* YOUNG MARY *lying on her bed in the blue
room, afraid, breathing deeply.*

MARY (*voice-over*): It is an utterly horrible feeling . . .

*We see her eyes, as she is sitting in the park. The images
are turning almost to black.*

I couldn't help myself . . .

*She lies down on the park bench. She stretches out, like her
younger self lying on the bed in the blue room, frightened.
She begins to cry uncontrollably, sobbing on the bench in
the park. Her whole body shaking.*

  *She suddenly realises a small girl of about ten is
standing watching her. But she can't stop herself crying.
The girl's mother suddenly appears and swoops her
daughter away, looking disapproving at this madwoman
in the park.*

  We see MARY *curled up tight now on the bench as she
continues to cry.*

  *We cut to a shot of her scurrying away down the hill in
the park, her shoulders hunched, as if she is trying to hide
in her own body, as she attempts to get out of the park.*

I ran away . . . I ran away from the park.

INT. SIXTIES ROOM. NIGHT

MARY *wipes away a couple of tears from her cheeks. She has
managed to stop herself breaking down in front of* JOE. *She
smiles slightly, pulling herself together, sitting very straight.*

MARY: It was disgraceful, Joe . . . my exhibition. Crying for
  one's youth – what a useless thing to do! But at least –
  (*Her tone stronger.*) That feeling of things being shut

down . . . of it all ending . . . I fought that . . . (*She smiles.*) He didn't manage that . . . !

She looks up at JOE.

MARY: And somehow I forced myself here . . . something I've been thinking about for years – to come back here, confront the place. I even phoned up once or twice . . . but I never had the courage.

She stands up.

Today, after the park, I just walked straight here . . . it seemed the obvious thing to do. And you were kind enough to let me in . . .

JOE: You came to . . . ? To see if he was here?

MARY: To see if I could get rid of a ghost – which isn't a ghost, of course. Not a proper ghost.

MARY *leaves the room.* JOE *follows her.*

JOE: And have you . . . ? (*He catches up with her.*) Have you?

MARY: I'm sorry, I've got to go now, Joe.

JOE: You have, haven't you . . . ? Got rid of him?

Pause.

MARY: Yes.

JOE: Promise me?

MARY (*hesitates, quieter*): Yes . . . (*She continues to move off.*) You don't need to show me out, I know the way . . . Just got to get out of this house!

JOE *is following her. She is disappearing fast down one of the passages. He calls after her.*

JOE: Are you going to the park tomorrow?

MARY *keeps moving, but she calls back.*

MARY: I might do!

JOE: Can I come too? See where it happened?

MARY *turns right at the end of the passage.*

MARY: See if he is still there, you mean . . . ? (*She calls.*) Eleven o'clock . . . ! (*She is disappearing down the passage.*) I hope I'll turn up . . .

JOE *is moving after her.*

JOE: Which park? You haven't told me which park?!

    MARY *rounds the corner of the passage and is gone. We hear her voice.*

MARY: Kensington Gardens.

EXT. PARK. DAY

We see JOE *standing alone on a broad path.*

JOE (*voice-over*): She had given me the time, and the park – but not where she'd be . . . ! I looked and looked for her. I didn't find her . . . And then at last, just when I was going, there she was!

    We see MARY *standing some distance away on the broad path. She looks elegant again, as when she first came through the door.*

MARY: Hello, Joe . . . here I am. You didn't think I'd come . . .

    Time cut. We are tracking with MARY *and* JOE *along the path, up the hill.*

JOE (*voice-over*): We walked in silence. She didn't seem to want to talk.

    We see him glancing sideways at her.

I don't know what she was thinking . . .

    We stay on MARY *as she walks.*

    We cut to MARY *and* JOE *reaching the alcove with the bench.*

JOE: Is this the spot?

MARY: This is the spot.

    They both sit on the bench, with a little space between them.

JOE (*voice-over*): I still didn't know what to say . . . So I didn't say anything.

MARY (*suddenly*): You can go now, Joe. Thank you for staying. I'm OK . . . It'll be fine . . . I'll be fine.

JOE *gets up. She smiles at him.*

MARY: You helped me.

JOE: Right . . .

MARY: But I just need to be on my own . . .

JOE *hesitates.*

MARY: You can leave me, Joe, it's OK. I promise.

JOE (*voice-over*): So I left her there. And she did seem better. I think.

We see him staring back at her from a distance.

She was sitting there, looking quite elegant, reading a book, when I left her.

JOE *takes one more look at her. She does look better. He hesitates again, wondering if he should call out to her. Then he leaves.*

INT. STAIRCASE/FIRST-FLOOR PASSAGE. DAY

We cut to the camera moving up the stairwell and discovering JOE *sitting in the middle of the first-floor passage listening to his Discman. The image we first saw of him.*

JOE (*voice-over*): I keep thinking about her . . . things I still want to ask. I'll go back tomorrow to the park, but I expect she won't be there . . . (*He looks up.*) There was something about her . . . I liked that lady.

EXT. PARK. DAY

We are tracking away from MARY *as she sits on her own, reading on the park bench.*

JOE (*voice-over*): I hope she never sees him again.

We stay on MARY *as she sits in the park.*

Fade to black.

A REAL SUMMER

A Real Summer was produced by BBC Television and was first screened in November 2007. The cast was as follows:

Young Mary	Ruth Wilson
Geraldine	Ruth Wilson

Writer/Director Stephen Poliakoff
Executive Producer Eddie Morgan
Music Adrian Johnston
Director of Photography Danny Cohen
Film Editor Tom Kinnersley
Production Designer Madelaine Leech

YOUNG MARY *is sitting in a fifties dress on a settee. Three Dalmatian dogs are keeping her company.* YOUNG MARY *is addressing us, staring straight at the lens.*

YOUNG MARY: Normally I know how to start any article
I write, any column, because I won't even sit down
to write until I have the opening sentence planned.
But beginning this – which is a rather strange story – is
difficult because it started in such an unexpected way.
A big wide shot of the room with YOUNG MARY *seemingly
miles away from us. We realise we are in the very large
reception room of a grand house.*
And as I sit thinking about this column I am in
somebody else's house, a rather magnificent house in
fact, surrounded by three Dalmatians. The dogs belong
to a person I hardly know, but who has had a most
peculiar effect on me. How has this come about?
YOUNG MARY *stares down at the dogs for a moment and
then back at us.*
When you are a film critic you don't tend to get invited
to an awful lot of parties by people in the entertainment
industry, because they are, rather understandably,
very wary of you. Some of them hate you. They greet
you with frozen smiles, talk only about the most
neutral of subjects such as the amount of rain this
summer and the difficulty of finding taxis, and then
they scuttle away as soon as they can.

But since I have given up being a critic and started
this column I have found myself altogether more
popular – invited to all sorts of places . . .
*We see archive travelling shots down leafy Buckinghamshire
lanes.*

*One of those being Pinewood Studios, the heart of the
British film industry.*

We see shots of the studio gates with the commissionaires

in smart uniforms, we see shots of men in suits and ties manoeuvring huge lights, people painting scenery, film directors smoking pipes sitting with young actresses crouched at their feet. We hear YOUNG MARY*'s voice over the images.*

I was determined to be on my best behaviour, merely observe, and not start any argument about the insularity of British films which I know I have railed about week after week with tedious regularity.

More images of the studio. We cut back to YOUNG MARY.

I thought I would be entering a very hierarchical world – film directors arriving in their chauffeur-driven Bentleys with commissionaires doffing their caps to them or saluting like feudal servants on a great country estate . . . and young actresses being treated with patronising jollity by these same directors. 'No, darling, that's not how you do it, surely you can pick up a cigarette lighter and talk at the same time . . . ?!' A little wink at the surrounding male technicians, and then the film director rolls his eyes and sighs: 'I'll have to show you, darling, won't I?' YOUNG MARY *stares straight at the lens.*

And disappointingly that is precisely what I found. Except more so. And naturally my silence didn't last long.

Travelling shots through the studio buildings. Then we cut back to YOUNG MARY.

At lunch in their panelled boardroom we were served some particularly leathery roast beef. Maybe it was the experience of trying to cut this meat, which had the consistency of a wellington boot, but suddenly I heard myself asking the assembled film-makers and producers whether they were ever tempted to leave the safety of the studio and the pretty Pinewood garden in which several thousand exterior scenes have been shot – and shoot an entire film on location, like some Italian and American directors had done. 'Go to an industrial city or the wilds of Northumberland,' I urged. Incredulity spread across the dining room. It was as if I had suggested my own mother direct the film about the sinking of the *Titanic* that is currently in production.

'You must understand,' they said, talking very slowly, 'how films are *really* made – all the lights that are required, the stars' dressing rooms . . . how impossible that would be, *a whole film* on location!' They roared with laughter. They were still laughing when the rice pudding with apricot jam was served.

One of the producers leans towards me as he eats his dessert. 'It is the story that matters, surely you know that? Why should you care where something is shot or what the Italians and Americans are doing?'

Put on the defensive, I am afraid I muttered the fatal words – very pompous, I know – 'I care what they are doing because I am passionate about cinema.' This was greeted with one of the most embarrassed silences I've ever heard – it was as if I had come out with a volley of obscenities. The word 'passionate' uttered in the boardroom of Pinewood Studios! Surely not?!

We see colour archive footage now, travelling shots through the Buckinghamshire countryside. Large mock-Tudor mansions and summer gardens.

After that I was in a hurry to get away, but there was a cocktail party at a film producer's house and Cary Grant was expected, travelling all the way from Elstree Studios where he is making the movie *Indiscreet*. The film producer's house was quite near the studios, a large mock-Tudor mansion, but with a very exotic garden full of azaleas in bloom and strong, almost tropical smells. A more exciting, more romantic garden, by the way, than I had ever seen in a British movie. But naturally there is no sign of Cary Grant . . .

Suddenly I'm approached by a young woman, let us call her Felicity, although that is not her name. She is about my own age, has an open pretty face. She says she hasn't the faintest idea why she's here in this garden with all these people from the film world, why she's been invited – she hasn't the foggiest clue, it can only be a mistake! She asked me who I was and what I did.

'Oh, you must be frightfully brainy,' she said.

Modesty demanded that at least I tried to deny this.

'No, no, you're obviously so brainy and that's marvellous,' she insists. 'I like clever people,' she giggles. 'Actually, I don't meet very many! . . . As for me, I am a real dunce, I can't hide it, so I just admit it!' She was laughing away merrily, almost boastfully. Suddenly her face is quite close, her pale blue eyes studying me. 'How do you choose what to write about in your column every week . . . ?'

I'm often asked this, and I try my best to be vague, because the truth is embarrassingly chaotic and last-minute. So I was just about to give my usual evasive answer when she said, 'Why don't you write about me?'

This I was not expecting.

'Write about you . . . ?' I can't quite keep the amazement out of my voice. 'Yes!' she beams at me.

I have to admit it is rare for me not to know what to say next . . . Eventually I manage a blank, non-committal, 'I don't normally write about specific people . . . '

Felicity is not impressed by this argument.

'Don't you? Why ever not? Then you should start with a dimwit like me – because if you can make me

interesting then you really would be a good writer.'
YOUNG MARY *pauses.*

What do you say to something like that? I was trying
hard not to be rude, and yet I knew I had to get rid
of her. But for some reason all I could manage was a
feeble, 'I would need to know more about you before
I could . . . ' Felicity seizes on this.

'That's easy! Let's have tea then. I am sure you are
frightfully busy but maybe you can fit in a tiny tea
with me . . . ?!'

We see two of the Dalmatian dogs looking at YOUNG
MARY *enquiringly from across the room. Their eyes full of
surprise.*

*We then see archive footage of London street scenes in
the fifties, ladies in hats having tea in the tea rooms of
large London hotels such as the Waldorf.*

We cut back to YOUNG MARY *sitting in another part of
the atmospheric reception room. She is surrounded by tea
things. She is drinking tea from a beautiful tea service and
there are biscuits and fruit and little sandwiches on a silver
stand.*

YOUNG MARY: So I find myself having a tiny tea in Fuller's
in Knightsbridge. Felicity is eating a bright pink
strawberry ice cream; she has asked for two extra
wafers and she is eating these first, munching quite
loudly. She totally ignores the melting ice cream. In
between munches, she suddenly asks, 'Do you have a
husband, or a boyfriend, or a scrumptious lover of
some sort?' I said, not at the moment.

YOUNG MARY *bites on a biscuit.*

There is a pause, and Felicity's face clouds over. 'I was
nearly married – I was engaged, but then I discovered
he was still rogering about four of his ex-girlfriends.
At *least* four! And he was clearly not going to let a little
thing like a wedding with me stop him. My family

were very disappointed – he was thought of as quite a catch, a real deb's delight. They didn't think his bottom going up and down in lots of different bedrooms all over London was nearly a strong enough reason for stopping the marriage!' She laughed her merry laugh. 'So I am on the proverbial shelf.' She points at the coffee-shop counter as if that is the precise spot where she is going to spend the rest of her life. She waves her wafer. 'My sister Georgina is about to come out. You know this is the last season, the *last time* the debs are going to be presented to the Queen. Isn't that extraordinary – they are stopping it after all this time?'

She stares at me, as if this is one of the most cataclysmic events in European history. 'Were you presented to the Queen?' I ask unnecessarily. Her face lights up.

'Oh yes – all of us virgins sitting in Buckingham Palace in neat rows, and then curtseying to the Queen.'
We see archive of a gaggle of swan-like debs descending the stairs at the Queen Charlotte's Ball in their white dresses. We hear Felicity's voice over the images:
'And then curtsying in front of the giant cake at the Queen Charlotte's Ball – isn't that just completely crackers, all these women and a large cake! And when you finally got to eat it – it turned out just to be a horrible old fruit cake!'
We cut back to YOUNG MARY.
And then she is off, prattling on about her life as a deb, all the dances and balls in these great houses, the floodlit gardens, the incredible time and effort that went into arranging the whole thing . . . the desperation of the mothers . . .
We see archive images of houses and gardens at night and debs moving in their long dresses.

The terrible fear of rejection if you didn't get enough partners during each night, the dreamlike nature of it all because you were so short of sleep all the time . . .

'You felt like you were both floating and drowning at the same time!' she chirps.

She starts on her third wafer. By this time her ice cream has completely melted and she hasn't touched it.

I can't decide if she is one of the silliest people I have ever met – which is indeed what she claims – or if there is something else going on. If there is another side to her. Why on earth does she want me to write about her?

We cut to the Dalmatians moving a little nearer to YOUNG MARY *and staring up at her eagerly.*

'My father's a duke,' Felicity suddenly says, looking straight at me – and then, as if willing me to look disapproving, she adds, 'I'm afraid that is the case . . . Not a really really big duke,' she giggles, 'although he is quite tall – more a sort of middling one, quite an ancient title, you know, with all the usual things that come with that – the big house in the country, lots of dogs and a terrifying old nanny. Nanny Luckham. She taught me practically nothing except how to make queen's pudding – which is in fact quite difficult.'

Slight pause.

'She was a better cook than the cook. That is what she should have been doing. All sorts of things might have been different . . . '

She stares for a long moment at her last wafer, as she contemplates the badly organised servants.

'What does your father do?' she asks, still staring at the wafer.

I tell her the truth, that he is a carpenter. She is completely stunned. 'Oh my goodness . . . ! Really? Are you being serious?'

I can't resist piling it on because I know my northern background will make it even worse.

'Yes, a carpenter in Manchester. That is where I was brought up.'

Felicity takes a moment to digest this. It is as if she had known I was different, but not that different, and maybe this was too much to handle, and the tea should come to an abrupt end. After due consideration she decides to let it continue . . . and she wants to hear all about my scholarship to Oxford, when I lost my Manchester accent, how my parents view me now. And she keeps interjecting, 'You're even brainier than I thought you were! . . . And here I am knowing simply nothing!'

I think maybe I should at least try to contradict this for politeness' sake, but for the first time Felicity becomes quite forceful.

'No – it is true. I know absolutely nothing. I promise you.' Her eyes are fierce. She won't be contradicted. I have to nod and agree with her. Her voice softens.

'I *could* have known more . . . I met George Bernard Shaw for instance, I sat on his knee when he came to stay with us . . . I went to Queen Mary's funeral with my father, because my mother was away in the country – and I met the Duke of Windsor there. You know the royal family had a meal that night all together and they never invited him. The day of his own mother's funeral! How could they have done that? Mind you, he's meant to be thicker than me!'

She pauses after giving me this little royal anecdote. She stares in surprise at her melted ice cream and licks the spoon. She then leans towards me and fixes me with an intense look. She says slowly, 'Somebody at that party said you were very pleased with yourself . . . '

Pause.

I try to take this in my stride, probably not very
successfully, because there is undoubtedly a shred
of truth in it. So I mutter something along the line,
'I really hope I don't give that impression . . . '

Felicity continues to peer at me.

'*I* don't think it's true,' she finally pronounces, and
then she smiles. 'You said you were passionate about
cinema. That made them very cross, very cross indeed.'
She laughs. 'I'm glad you did . . . ! What a wonderful
thing to be – passionate!'

Suddenly her face is very close, and her tone is
almost urgent.

'You know, I have never been to a foreign film.
Ever! Will you take me to one . . . ?'

I hesitate. The very last thing I want to do is act as
a one-woman finishing school for this ex-deb.

Her eyes are pleading with me.

'Please, Mary. Do that for me . . . !'

*Shots of fifties traffic in the rain in London, steam trains
pulling into stations, people scuttling along the streets past
dark buildings which are still showing their wartime
shabbiness.*

We cut to YOUNG MARY *sitting in a different place in
the room. A table lamp is switched on next to her, she is
throwing a shadow on the wall. The rest of the room is
bathed in a late-afternoon light, the sun is just beginning
to dip.*

So I take her to a little cinema tucked away behind
Paddington Station. I had no idea what sort of
'foreign' film she wanted to see – so I had decided on
Henri-Georges Clouzot's *Les Diaboliques* – a strong
story, I told myself, one that was easy to follow . . .

We move in on YOUNG MARY*'s face in the shadow of the
room.*

As we approach the cinema a thunderstorm suddenly explodes over the dark streets of Paddington. And inside, the auditorium is almost empty except for three strange-looking men, two of them grotesquely fat. So the atmosphere is a little eerie even before the film begins.

We see the eyes of the ornaments in the room, the china animals on the mantelpiece and the portraits, staring at YOUNG MARY, *expectantly, watchfully.*

Just as the movie starts, one of the grotesques comes and sits right behind us wheezing and blowing smoke against our necks.

The dogs are watching YOUNG MARY *now.*

Those of you who have seen *Les Diaboliques* will know it casts a spell of extraordinary evil, rancid and claustrophobic. I have to admit even though I have seen it three times and know the twist, I still find it quite frightening.

The eyes of the portraits staring at her.

About halfway through Felicity clasps hold of my arm, holding it so tight it hurts, and she doesn't let go until the end of the film. She is like a child on a rollercoaster.

We are close on YOUNG MARY*'s eyes.*

When there is a particularly nasty murder, somebody being held down in a bath, she lets out a little mew-like cry.

Pause on YOUNG MARY. *She lets out the cry.*

And when we creep around the house near the end of the film, and visit another bath, and see a corpse rise from under the water which causes the heroine to have a fatal heart attack, I feel Felicity's breathing get faster and faster, and I glance at her and her eyes are full of terror – I don't think I've ever seen anybody look quite so afraid.

We see YOUNG MARY*'s eyes full of terror.*

We cut wide. YOUNG MARY *leans over and takes a cigarette out of a silver cigarette case on a little ornamental table beside her. She lights it.*

Even before the lights come up, I feel terrible. I have punished her for asking for my help by taking her to the most terrifying film I could find in a seedy cinema where we are menaced by ghoulish men sitting right behind us.

The big eyes of the dogs stare at her reproachfully.

On the pavement outside, as the rain lashes down, Felicity turns towards me. She is standing without an umbrella, getting completely soaked, her eyes are shining. 'Mary . . . ! That was the most wonderful film I have ever seen! It was fantastic . . . it was completely gorgeous!'

We walk in the rain for a little while. I have a strong sense what her next question is going to be – and I know I am going to say yes. She stops and looks straight at me. 'We can't – can we? – go to another flick together . . . ? Or maybe a play . . . ? Something new and different . . . ? I've heard about these new sort of plays with lavatories onstage and ironing boards and people boiling kettles . . . !'

I realise I am going to spend a few more days with Felicity. She has obviously decided I am going to be her own private guide to this new world and I find it impossible to say no. I have to admit – and you've already guessed this – I was getting rather intrigued by her, although I can't quite work out why. There is a loneliness there obviously but also a hunger and a sense of fun.

Archive footage of society garden parties, Royal Ascot, etc.

So during this last season, as the debs are being presented for their final curtsies to the Queen, Felicity and I go on an alternative season, an orgy of avant-garde work. We see a play at the Royal Court about a working-class family with a very provocative title, *Live Like Pigs*. We go and see Ingmar Bergman's *Wild Strawberries*, which has been such a critical sensation this month, we see a play at Stratford East by a nineteen-year-old girl from Salford, Shelagh Delaney, called *A Taste of Honey*, which is amazing, and we see a rather good amateur production of *Waiting for Godot*. 'I think Godot must be rather like my doctor,' pronounces Felicity. 'He always says he will pop round, but he usually finds an excuse not to!'

We see archive of a film premiere, many British stars of the period being photographed in the foyer.

I also take Felicity to a royal gala premiere of a British war film where she can see all Pinewood's finest on display. (*She smiles.*) I hear her voice ringing out loudly across the foyer of the Empire, Leicester Square, before the film starts, just as Jack Hawkins walks past. ' I have a new love in my life, this adorable mad Irishman – Mr Samuel Beckett!'

Travelling shots going down Park Lane. We see the great hotels and the mansions that still lined it in the 1950s.

And all the time she is anxious to show me bits of her world. We drive along Park Lane and watch the debs pouring into their balls, and stare through lighted windows at all the decorations, and see the partygoers drunkenly throwing bits of food and clothing out of the window of their hotel suites onto the heads of the passers-by below.

Four days ago we were just coming out of a special press preview of Mr Hitchcock's *Vertigo* – a very dark and dreamlike film about obsessive love, when Felicity turns to me. 'Well, Mary,' she says, ' I think you have changed my life. And I am sure that's a good thing, in fact I *know* that's an absolutely splendid thing! . . . And so I should give you a present . . . '

I remonstrate. 'No, no, that's not necessary. It's been really good to see some of these films and plays again, watch them with new eyes, and to discover some totally fresh things too . . . '

Felicity is staring straight at me. 'Good,' she says firmly. 'So you won't mind very much then – I know this is monstrous of me – if I ask you for yet another favour? Do you mind? Well, here goes anyway! I have to go down to the country this week, my sister is having her big coming-out ball there. And here in London I have three dogs, Dalmatians actually. Augustus, Beatrice and Tilly. I love Dalmatians – *A Hundred and One Dalmatians* is one of my favourite books. And I don't want them to be alone for two days. You see, in London we have hardly any servants now, can't really afford to run two big houses any more! My grandfather died suddenly in an accident, and my father became Duke very fast, and had to move to the country, and everything is a bit of a muddle – and my dogs very definitely don't get on with the dogs in the country. And I don't want to leave them with just two grumpy chambermaids to look after them . . . 'Could *you* stay with them for two days?' She is imploring me with her big eyes. 'I mean, you might find it interesting, our house. You could poke around, find things to write about. And the chambermaids won't be grumpy with *you*!'

I am speechless, utterly speechless. Her face is thrust close to mine, waiting for my answer. I realise here is somebody who is so used to getting what they want . . . For that reason alone I am trying my hardest to say no.

We see a wide shot of the big reception room. YOUNG
MARY *is now in a different dress, rather more formal and
she is surrounded by three Dalmatians. A grandfather
clock is ticking. The light is magic-hour, dusk streaked with
bits of sun.*

So that is how I have ended up in this room, surrounded
by Dalmatians. Somehow in the space of three weeks,
after a chance meeting, Felicity has scooped me up,
claimed hours and hours of my time and now deposited
me in her house, waited on by silent servants. And
I have even put on my very best dress, as if I was
attending a great society occasion when in fact I am
here all on my own! How has she managed to compel
me to do all this? There is something about her that
suggests –

The phone rings. YOUNG MARY *looks at it for a second,
as if wondering if she should answer it, this not being her
house. Then she picks it up.*

We cut to FELICITY/GERALDINE. *She is standing in a
magnificent ball gown. She is on the phone in a passage.
She is in half-shadow. At the end of the passage we can
see a glowing light. Her tone is edgier than Felicity's.*

GERALDINE: Hello, Mary.

YOUNG MARY: Hello, Geraldine. Here I am with the dogs.

GERALDINE: Good.

YOUNG MARY: This house is *amazing* . . .

GERALDINE: I've been reading your column. You are
making me sound too sensible. You haven't caught my
full silliness . . .

YOUNG MARY: Oh, I don't know about that! (*She smiles.*)
I am doing my best.

GERALDINE: And why did you call me Felicity?

YOUNG MARY: It is just a name. I needed a name.

GERALDINE: You could have chosen a prettier name. How
  are the dogs?
YOUNG MARY: The dogs are well. I think at least Augustus
  quite likes me.

GERALDINE (*sharp*): Augustus likes everybody. He has no
    judgement at all.
    Slight pause.

YOUNG MARY: Are you all right, Geraldine? You sound . . .
    a little angry with me?

GERALDINE: No, no. I am just standing in the passage, in
    a dress I might wear tomorrow – I am trying out
    two or three tonight. Outside in the dark there are
    twenty little Greek temples specially built for the ball.
    Tomorrow they will all blaze with light . . . and it will
    be intoxicating and dreamlike . . .

YOUNG MARY: It sounds spectacular.

GERALDINE (*crisply*): I am sure it will be . . .
    *She sits on a chair in a passage. There is a table by her
    covered in magazines and old newspapers.*
    I am sitting now. (*Slight laugh.*) Could make all the
    difference . . .
    She picks up a carefully folded newspaper.
    My mother keeps all the Sunday newspapers for at
    least a year after they've appeared – she never seems
    to read them, but she never throws them out. So I've
    been able to read some of your old columns. You *are*
    very outspoken, aren't you, Mary?

YOUNG MARY: You mean rude.

GERALDINE: Like I'm reading here, 'Kenneth More has all
    the sex appeal of an old English sheepdog . . . If we
    are to compete with the Americans we have to find
    actors with real danger and not just constantly feature
    chuckling men who never seem to have been young.'
    Should you write about film actors like that, Mary?

YOUNG MARY: I don't see why not. But I agree it could be
    a little wittier . . .

GERALDINE: I like it how you blast everything, though –
    attacking lots of smug men. That's rather fun! You're

not exactly cruel – that's not quite right. You're
impatient, Mary . . . impatient for change . . .

YOUNG MARY: I am sure that's what I am, yes . . .

GERALDINE: I bet your friends are saying, 'Why are you
spending all that space writing about that silly young
aristo . . . what could have possessed you? You've
already spent two columns on her!' That's what they
are saying, aren't they – all your sophisticated friends?

YOUNG MARY: Nobody has said that. I am not sure
anybody is reading it – but nobody's said that!

GERALDINE: You're lying, Mary. You are not a very good
liar . . . do you know that?

YOUNG MARY: So people tell me!

GERALDINE: The truth is you got a bit fascinated with me
and yet you don't really know why.

YOUNG MARY (*calmly*): That is the truth, yes.

GERALDINE: Have you poked about in all my cupboards
yet? Like I told you? Tried on my shoes? I am sure we
have both got the same nice feet. Read my diary?
Have you?

YOUNG MARY: How do I answer that? You won't believe
me if I say no.

GERALDINE: So you have then!

YOUNG MARY: Not yet.

GERALDINE: Go ahead. Go on. Promise me you will . . .
YOUNG MARY *looks surprised.*

YOUNG MARY: If you insist . . . I promise.

GERALDINE: You know, I quite like the Felicity you created
in your column. It made me laugh. Some of it. When
we went off to see that play about the two queer
Italian trapeze artists – that was jolly! At the time it
was funny – but you made it funnier.

YOUNG MARY: Good.

GERALDINE (*suddenly intense*): BUT SHE IS NOT ME.

YOUNG MARY: Not completely. I've not got all of you . . .
not so far . . .

GERALDINE: You're a detective now, are you? (*Slight laugh.*)
Going to get to the bottom of things?
*There is a pause. We stay on her face; a look of grief passes
across it.*
Oh, Mary – if only I wasn't here. You can't imagine
what it's like . . .
GERALDINE *lets out a strange noise, a half-cry.*

YOUNG MARY: Geraldine . . . ? What is it?

GERALDINE: Got to go. Got to go, Mary . . . I'll call you
later. (*Suddenly intense.*) Be by the phone at eleven
o'clock. (*Her voice urgent.*) Be there for me. Mary . . .
We cut back to YOUNG MARY *ringing off and staring
down at the phone for a moment.*
 *Then we cut to her wandering alone through the room.
It is now dusk, the sun has set.*
 We cut to her opening drawers, going through
GERALDINE*'s things, glancing at letters.*
 *We cut to her sitting on a chair at the other end of the
room, with three pairs of* GERALDINE*'s shoes lined up. She
begins to try them on. Loud sound of a clock ticking.*
 We then cut to her trying on one of GERALDINE*'s Ascot
hats.*
 *We cut to a wide shot of the main reception room. It is
now night, and for a moment the room is empty.*
 YOUNG MARY *enters the room. She pauses, standing
framed in the doorway. The dogs are curled up in their
basket. They raise their heads as she comes in.* YOUNG
MARY *sits by the phone. It is eleven o'clock. We move in
on the phone. It does not ring. We dissolve.*
 YOUNG MARY *is kneeling by the dogs. The grandfather
clock shows it is now eleven thirty.*

YOUNG MARY (*looking down at the dogs*): She's late . . . Why
am I concerned about her, Augustus? I don't know

why I should think anything is the matter. Anything more than she's a bit sad today, a bit melancholic . . . I don't know why I am really worried about her. (*She smiles.*) But I must be, mustn't I – because I am talking to you!

We cut to YOUNG MARY *just finishing dialling on the phone.*

Is that Kelverton? This is Mary Gilbert . . . I just wondered if I could talk to Geraldine, please?

We hear a muffled noise at the other end. An old man's voice.

Sorry . . . ? What did you say? Hold on? Right . . .
*She looks across at the dogs as she waits. She addresses
them.*
Have you ever been there? I'm imagining some huge
old spooky house . . .
There is a muffled male voice on the phone.
Hello? What? You can't find her? . . . What do you
mean, she has either left or is in the East Wing? Can't
you go and look for her in the East Wing?
Sound of the muffled male voice.
Who am I talking to? What? Mr Jeffrey . . . ? And you
are . . . ? The butler . . . Right . . . Could you, Mr
Jeffrey, if you see Geraldine by any chance in the East
Wing, tell her to ring Mary . . .
She rings off. She addresses the dogs.
The East Wing is probably two miles long . . . (*She
smiles at the dogs.*) Patrolled by hundred-year-old
retainers.

We cut to YOUNG MARY *sitting at a desk in the corner of the room. It is now one thirty. She slides a book out from among the papers on the desk. She opens it. We move in on the first page.*

'This is Geraldine's Diary,' *it says.*

She turns another page. 'To whoever is looking . . . by all means read!'

She turns another page. 'My Last Diary.'

We move in on YOUNG MARY's *face. She turns the other pages. They are all blank.*

The phone rings. YOUNG MARY *answers it.*

We cut to GERALDINE *lying on a four-poster bed in her petticoat. The room is very shadowy. We intercut between her and* YOUNG MARY *sitting on a high-backed chair.*

YOUNG MARY: Geraldine, there you are!

GERALDINE's *tone is dark.*

GERALDINE: What's the matter? Been missing me . . . ?

YOUNG MARY: No, no, I was just expecting you to ring . . . You sounded unhappy.

Pause. We are close on GERALDINE's *face.*

GERALDINE: *You* scared me.

YOUNG MARY: I scared you? When?

GERALDINE: With that film. That terrifying French movie – you really scared me.

YOUNG MARY: I shouldn't have done that, no. I'm sorry.

GERALDINE: No, you shouldn't. (*Very slight pause.*) We had some good times, though, after that.

YOUNG MARY: We did. Geraldine . . . you sound very low. Is there something I can do?

GERALDINE: Like what?

YOUNG MARY: I don't know. Help in some way?

GERALDINE: You want something, an answer, a secret . . . but there isn't anything, Mary. Not anything big. Just a series of small, not very special puddles.

YOUNG MARY: Puddles? What do you mean?

GERALDINE: Some not very heroic incidents . . . that's
what I mean. My grandfather didn't die in an accident,
of course – he shot himself two years ago. He was
almost naked, the gun in his mouth, never told
anybody why. But then you had guessed that had
happened, hadn't you?

YOUNG MARY: Maybe . . .

GERALDINE: Both him and my father are silent – *were*
very, very silent . . . My father is even more silent
now. I watched him tonight; he's losing his daughter,
Georgina – she's going to marry the first deb's delight
that kisses her breast, you just know that'll happen . . .
and he is losing her. But he'll never say anything,
never say, 'I love you, darling.'
We move slowly in on her.
When I was fifteen I came upon my father and
grandfather sitting on the floor in the library. They had
been looking at some pictures and there they were,
sitting on the floor in total silence. Like measuring
their respective lives out in silent chunks. I think there
is every chance my father will go the same way as my
grandfather, not quite yet but one day –

YOUNG MARY (*softly*): Geraldine, I am sure that won't
happen –

GERALDINE*'s voice is intense.*

GERALDINE: And you know what really scares me? – I
think, where will it stop? . . . What about Georgina's
boy, when she has a boy . . . will it go on and on . . . ?
My grandfather was in the First World War, my father
in the Second, so maybe that's got something to do
with it – war. But I don't know about that, Mary –
maybe they *never* would have talked, whatever
happened. They made the world slow down so much
by never saying anything . . . When I was growing up
I screamed for each week to end.

YOUNG MARY (*softly*): But that's finished now –

GERALDINE (*sharply*): Has it?

    She stares out for a moment

    I missed my chance, Mary. I'll never forgive myself for
    that.

YOUNG MARY: Why did you miss your chance?

GERALDINE: You going to write about this?

YOUNG MARY: No, of course not.

GERALDINE: Really? Is Felicity suddenly going to turn into a troubled mad aristo?

YOUNG MARY: I'm not going to write about this.

GERALDINE: How are you going to end her then, if you don't use this?

YOUNG MARY: I'll think of a way –

GERALDINE: Of course you'll write about it, because writers are cold – cold, cold, cold.

YOUNG MARY: That is undoubtedly true, Geraldine . . . but I'll never write about this conversation because it wouldn't fit . . . My Felicity was very frivolous and you aren't . . . Remember, though, you *wanted* me to write about you . . .

GERALDINE: That's right . . . but then I knew you'd write about me the way you did . . .

YOUNG MARY (*softly*): What was the opportunity you missed, Geraldine?

GERALDINE: It's nothing very much . . . I missed a golden chance.

When I was tiny, before the war, there was a house, a magical house in the middle of London, Holland House . . .

We see archive images of this magnificent Jacobean house in its own parkland in the middle of 1930s Kensington.
It is now a ruin in the middle of Holland Park, but then it was like a castle in a fairy story. And just a few weeks before war broke out there was a great ball attended by everybody that was anybody, the King and Queen, foreign princes, prime ministers, Noël Coward too!

I was only five. Of course I didn't go to the ball, but I overheard everybody talking about it . . . and my nanny had shown me the house!

We see limousines moving through the night.

It was raining the night of the ball, and for some
reason I wanted to stay awake, to hear them come
back. And I heard the voice of my father down the
passage . . . and suddenly the door of my bedroom is
opening and there he is, standing there, very tall and
handsome, and he is soaked from head to foot and he
looks so happy. The only time I ever remember him
really smiling. My parents had been so exhilarated by
the night, they had left the chauffeur and the car and
walked all the way back in the rain. The ball had been
that magical . . . ! And my father comes over to me –
and his face is very close and he says: 'My angel, my
little angel . . . '

YOUNG MARY: That's nice – so he did put it into words –

GERALDINE: Don't get sentimental on me, Mary – I was in
fact quite a fat little child, rather ugly, not the skinny
thing I am now. You've got to imagine this podgy
child lying there.

YOUNG MARY: I'm imagining that . . .

GERALDINE: And I am under the sheets and I remember
it so clearly – I nearly, *so very nearly*, stretch out my
little fist and touch his wet cheek . . . But for some
reason I didn't. I can't understand why I didn't . . .

YOUNG MARY: What difference would that have made?

GERALDINE: You're a fool if you don't see that. It would
have made all the difference. He remembers the ball –
but he doesn't remember coming in to see me . . . If
I had raised my hand – he wouldn't have forgotten
that! If I'd touched him . . . Because we *never, ever*
touch . . .

YOUNG MARY: Of course he remembers coming in and
staring down at you –

GERALDINE: He doesn't remember doing that – I KNOW
THAT FOR A FACT.

She stares into the dark. For a moment there is silence.

Everybody's life changed after that ball. For ever. The war came just a few weeks later. Then the house was bombed. We were told nothing would be the same again. In some ways that's true.

But then here I am, all this time later, lying on this bed, the night before another ghastly ball. Everybody going through the motions. The world doesn't seem to have changed after all . . . I don't know how that's really possible. How we've let that happen.

GERALDINE *gets up and moves into the shadow of the room.*

YOUNG MARY: Geraldine, are you still there? Geraldine?!

GERALDINE *gets back on the bed in a winter coat as if sheltering from the cold, even though it is summer.*

GERALDINE *then picks up the phone. She pauses.*

GERALDINE: I'm still here.

YOUNG MARY: You must get away from there, Geraldine. Start doing something different, all the new interests you have discovered over the last few weeks. Remember?

GERALDINE: That sounds nice and simple. And no doubt it will happen.

GERALDINE *gets up and moves into the shadows of the room.*

YOUNG MARY: Geraldine, are you still there? Geraldine?!

GERALDINE *gets back on the bed in a winter coat as if sheltering from the cold, even though it is summer.*

GERALDINE *then picks up the phone. She pauses.*

GERALDINE: I'm still here . . .

Anyway you mustn't worry about me, Mary, under any circumstances. And do you know why?

YOUNG MARY: I'm not worrying, but tell me why.

GERALDINE: Because I am going to marry a rich Argentinian. I fancy living in South America . . .

I haven't met him yet, but I can see him clearly and
I am sure I will come across him soon . . .

YOUNG MARY: That sounds terrific –

GERALDINE: It is. But the real reason you mustn't worry
about me, Mary, is – I am much more concerned
about *you*.

YOUNG MARY: About me? Why on earth are you concerned
about me?

GERALDINE: I will tell you, but I know you won't listen to
me.

YOUNG MARY: I will listen –

GERALDINE: You are lying again. Are we friends, Mary?
Tell me honestly.

YOUNG MARY: In a way.

GERALDINE: Yes, in a way. That's good. That's a good way
of putting it. Because we are hardly going to see each
other. In fact, you don't need to stay until I am back
on Monday. So it is possible we will never, ever see
each other again.

YOUNG MARY: I am sure that is not going to happen.

GERALDINE: *It is* what will happen.

YOUNG MARY: If you insist . . . So why are you worried
about me?

GERALDINE: Because you are brave and terribly, terribly
clear about everything. But maybe in a way – in a quite
different way to me – you are foolish too. Be careful,
won't you? It's not a time to take stupid risks . . .

YOUNG MARY: I won't take stupid risks.

GERALDINE: Not everybody likes to be seen clearly. You
are the one that will make enemies . . . You should
listen to me . . .

YOUNG MARY: I am . . .

GERALDINE (*with feeling*): I would hate something to happen
to you. We may not see each other again – but I will

be thinking of you . . . *often.* Be careful, Mary . . . Be
careful, won't you?
We stay on a close-up of GERALDINE. *Her face disappears
into darkness.*

And then we cut to YOUNG MARY *and move in on her
eyes.*

Fade to black.